Having Heaven on Earth in Your Marriage:

Answers for Developing Intimacy With Your Spouse

Having Heaven on Earth in Your Marriage:

Answers for Developing Intimacy With Your Spouse

by

Mack and Brenda Timberlake

Harrison House
Tulsa, Oklahoma

Having Heaven on Earth in Your Marriage:
Answers for Developing Intimacy With Your Spouse
ISBN 0-89274-641-8
Copyright © 1993
Christian Faith Center
P. O. Box 100
Creedmoor, North Carolina 27522

Published by Harrison House, Inc.
P. O. Box 35035
Tulsa, Oklahoma 74153

Contents

Introduction

When you got married, the person you married became your perfect mate. It doesn't matter what it looks like, you are married, and it's time to make it heaven on earth in your home.

Throughout the Scriptures, God tells us how to respond to one another in marriage. He used His relationship with Israel as an example in the Old Testament and Jesus and the Church in the New Testament.

Salvation is a marriage relationship between Jesus and the Church. Jesus became the spiritual husband to every person, whether male or female, when they became born again, when they asked Him to come into their heart. **For thy Maker is thine husband; the Lord of hosts is His name** (Isa. 54:5).

Read here what the Word of God says about the correlation between the marriage of a man and woman and the marriage of Jesus and the Church. There is only one set of standards for both of them.

Submitting yourselves one to another in the fear of God.

Wives, submit yourselves unto your own husbands, as unto the Lord.

For the husband is the head of the wife, even as Christ is the head of the church: and He is the Savior of the body.

7

Therefore as the church is subject unto Christ, so let the wives be to their own husbands in every thing.

Husbands, love your wives, even as Christ also loved the church, and gave Himself for it;

That He might sanctify and cleanse it with the washing of water by the word...

So ought men to love their wives as their own bodies. He that loveth his wife loveth himself.

For no man ever yet hated his own flesh; but nourisheth and cherisheth it, even as the Lord the church:

For we are members of His body, of His flesh, and of His bones...

This is a great mystery: but I speak concerning Christ and the church.

Nevertheless let every one of you in particular so love his wife even as himself; and the wife see that she reverence her husband.

Ephesians 5:21-26,28-30,32,33

Jesus wants us to become intimate with Him. He describes Himself as our friend.

Greater love hath no man than this, that a man lay down his life for his friends.

Ye are My friends, if ye do whatsoever I command you.

Henceforth I call you not servants; for the servant knoweth not what his lord doeth: but I have called you friends....

John 15:13-15

Friendship is the ingredient that keeps a marriage together.

Unless a man knows how to love Jesus, he will never know how to love his wife. And a woman will never be able to submit to any man, unless she first learns how to submit to Jesus.

You cannot have good horizontal relationships until you have your vertical relationship with God intact. It is from the union with God that we are energized and receive the ability to love, as He loves us.

Your marriage partner should be your most intimate friend. It is our desire to share with you, in this book, knowledge from God that will help you come into that reality in your marriage relationship.

1
Intimacy Starts With Friendship

Most of the time couples are friends, or they think they are friends, before they get married. After they get married, somehow, they lose their friendship. What is a friend? A friend is somebody you know. You know people on different levels: some casually only by their names, some personally, and then some intimately. The friend that you know intimately should be your mate.

Someone wrote, "Have you ever noticed most people end up marrying their best friend?" That should tell us something. If a husband or wife has a friend better than the spouse, they're in trouble. This is why so many bosses run away with their secretaries and husbands run away with their wife's best friend. They have gotten to know each other and become close, intimate friends.

Intimate does not exclusively refer to a sexual relationship, although that is included; but intimacy in a friendship means a close relationship. Intimacy is having a close relationship with someone who deeply loves and appreciates you for all you are, regardless of your shortcomings and failures. It is unconditional. There are many marriages that operate on conditional love. They are based on conditions like, "I'll love you if you get me that living room suite, or if you give me sex when I want to have it." But that is not what an intimate friend is.

John 15:21 says, **This is My commandment, That ye love one another, as I have loved you.** How much does Jesus love us? He loves us without limit, unconditionally. Jesus is a friend to God and to us. A friend does things on commitment, not on condition. A friend doesn't worry about what he is going to get out of it.

We are supposed to pattern our love and our friendship after Jesus Christ. Verse 13 says, **Greater love hath no man than this, that a man lay down his life for his friends.** A person who truly loves has no limitations.

As husband and wife, we become intimate friends; but intimacy doesn't happen overnight. We don't believe in love at first sight. You can have the "hots" for someone when you see that person for the first time, but there is no way you can love them, because you don't know them. Intimacy has to be developed. In marriage relationships you have to work at being friends; you have to work at getting to know one another. And knowing the person is knowing the heart of that person, knowing the core of that person. It is a long process and some couples, even though they are living together and sleeping with each other, have not developed an intimate relationship.

Maybe you are married and realize that you aren't really friends with each other. You may need to backtrack. If you don't build your house with a strong foundation and let that foundation settle, it will not be sturdy. When contractors lay a foundation with cement, they don't immediately begin to put the wood and brick on top of the cement. They give the cement time to settle. They let it solidify. Conversing with one another helps you to solidify your relationship, because you are learning about one another.

In the marriage relationship, both people have to work at being friends. An important part of that friendship is complete acceptance and total forgiveness. It doesn't matter what offense a spouse commits, husbands and wives should walk in forgiveness with one another. They can't say, "I'm going to forgive, but I won't forget."

The Word of God says He forgives us of our sins, and they are washed away as far as the east is from the west. (Ps. 103:12.) He doesn't say He will forgive us, but He's still going to write it in the book. He says it is erased from the book. In John 15:12, God says we are supposed to love one another as Jesus loved us. He loved us so much that He not only forgave us, but He *erased* our sins.

This is one of the biggest keys to any relationship: forgiveness. Sometimes we are tempted to ask, as Peter asked Jesus,

> **Lord, how oft shall my brother (spouse) sin against me, and I forgive him? till seven times?**
>
> **Jesus saith unto him, I say not unto thee, Until seven times: but, Until seventy times seven.**
>
> Matthew 18:21,22

The Word says that if you cannot forgive those around you every day who trespass against you, then God will not forgive you. (Mark 11:25.) Ask God for help. Pray, "Father God, I ask for Your ability to forgive my mate, even as You have forgiven me."

When you don't allow instant forgiveness to be in your life, you allow torment to come in on you.

> The Kingdom of Heaven can be compared to a king who decided to bring his accounts up to date. In the process, one of his debtors was brought in who owed him $10,000,000! He couldn't pay, so the king ordered him sold for the debt, also his wife and children and everything he had.
>
> But the man fell down before the king, his face in the dust, and said, 'Oh, sir, be patient with me and I will pay it all.'
>
> Then the king was filled with pity for him and released him and forgave his debt.
>
> But when the man left the king, he went to a man who owed him $2,000 and grabbed him by the throat and demanded instant payment.
>
> The man fell down before him and begged him to give him a little time. 'Be patient and I will pay it,' he pled.
>
> But his creditor wouldn't wait. He had the man arrested and jailed until the debt would be paid in full.
>
> Then the man's friends went to the king and told him what had happened. And the king called before him the man he had forgiven and said, 'You evil-hearted wretch! Here I forgave you all that tremendous debt, just because you asked me to — shouldn't you have mercy on others, just as I had mercy on you?'
>
> Then the angry king sent the man to the torture chamber until he had paid every last penny due. So shall my heavenly Father do to you if you refuse to truly forgive your brothers.
>
> **Matthew 18:23-34** TLB

When you don't allow forgiveness to operate in your life — it doesn't matter what your partner has done — you will be tormented. You'll stop resting at night. Your body is used to having love flow through it. Love is what causes your body to have energy. Unforgiveness will drain your strength. Your ideas and creativity in life will close down because faith works by love, and your love is shut down.

Early in our marriage, Brenda did something — really quite innocently — and I held it against her for a long time. We had just moved to Durham from Fayetteville, and my cousin invited us to attend a track meet at Duke. We took fried chicken sandwiches and planned on a wonderful day.

Brenda's vision at that time was not really that good. She would see people at a distance and mistake them for someone else. She saw a young man standing down on the bleachers, waving.

She said, "That's Dr. ____," and waved back.

I said, "No, Brenda, it isn't."

He came up to where we were sitting, and she could see him better and she said, "Oh, I thought you were Dr. ____."

He said, "No." So, they introduced themselves. Then Brenda said, "This is my husband."

Mack was so mad, I could see fire coming out of his nose. I've always been a very friendly person. In fact, that's what drew him to me. I didn't know it was a problem to my husband. I tried to be cordial, so I asked the young man if he would like a chicken sandwich.

Brenda gave that "dude" my chicken sandwich. He ate it and enjoyed it! I was so mad, I didn't see any more of the track meet. And it took me a long time to get over it.

Don't let yourself get in that position. That's torment. Satan will constantly be saying to you, "Don't forgive. Don't do it."

It doesn't matter who is at fault. Somebody has to be willing to be the one who says, "I'm sorry."

That has always been easy for me; Mack thought it was too easy. He didn't think I was sincere. He would say, "You always say that, and you don't mean it." But I suffered most of my early life living around people who were bitter and resentful, people who were always holding a grudge.

I didn't want that for my marriage, so it was no problem for me to be the one to say, "I'm sorry," no matter which one of us had blown it. I determined to do whatever it took to reestablish the peace in our home. Sometimes, I had to literally jump on his back and wrestle him down to the floor. He'd be enjoying it all the time. I'd say, "You're going to give up and forgive me." He'd say, "Keep saying you're sorry." We'd wrestle and it wouldn't take very long before forgiveness flowed and our relationship was restored.

A woman wants her husband to say the words, "Honey, I'm sorry. Will you personally, please forgive me?" But if we're walking with God, the important thing is to go to each other and say, "Honey, it doesn't matter, I'm sorry."

When you mature in your relationship, each will easily forgive and then you'll be free to discuss what brought the situation to the level of anger, so we won't make that same mistake again. You can ask, "What caused you to get angry? How did I miss it?"

The devil would try to get us so we're not speaking to one another. He tries to give us a spirit of contention, jealousy, backbiting, and resentment. Those are spirits that want to linger on. Those spirits are like leeches. A leech is a worm that catches hold on your flesh and draws the blood — the very substance that you need to live — out of your body and destroys you.

Unforgiveness is like a microscopic parasite in you; a parasite that can only be seen through a microscope. A microscope has magnifying glasses that illuminate a thing hundreds of times so you can see it. The Word of God magnifies the things in our lives, and it will show us any area of unforgiveness so we can get rid of it.

• Always be honest with one another. Dishonesty destroys the opportunity for intimacy to be developed.

2
The Primary Element Is Confidence

The first element necessary in developing an intimate relationship is confidence in that person. We serve Jesus Christ because we have a confidence in Him. We pray to our Heavenly Father, because we have confidence in Him. This is the assurance. It's the trust. It's the faith that we have in Jesus, the closeness that we have in Jesus, because in years and months and days past when we have prayed to Him, He has not failed us. When we go to Jesus He never tells anybody our secrets.

The same kind of faith that we develop with Jesus will enter into our relationship with our mate. But if we don't develop a closeness with Jesus, then we are going to have a problem developing a closeness with our mates. There is no way you can fully relate to a mate unless you can relate to Jesus.

We become intimate friends by confiding in each other, having confidence in each other. But that confidence only comes after a time of sharing with one another and truly getting to know and trust one another. When you are intimate with a person, you are very close to that person. When God took Adam's rib and made Eve, Adam said,

This is now bone of my bones, and flesh of my flesh: she shall be called Woman, because she was taken out of Man.

19

> Therefore shall a man leave his father and his mother, and shall cleave unto his wife: and they shall be one flesh.
>
> **Genesis 2:23,24**

Now that's close! That means that nobody should know more about you than your mate. You should not tell your secrets or feelings about your mate to anyone other than your mate. It opens the door for the devil to come in if you confide in someone other than your mate about a weakness your partner has. And if that partner ever finds out about it, then you will have a hard time ever having intimacy with them because there will be a wall of distrust built up between the two of you.

You may need to ask God when the right time is to share certain things, but you are so close to that person that nothing is kept secret from each other, but you keep each other's secrets from everyone else.

Proverbs 16:28 says, **A foolish man soweth strife and a whisperer separates the best of friends.** A "whisperer" is a gossiper. Sometimes husbands are not intimate with their wives because when the husband shares something with his wife, she tells it to someone else. She becomes a "whisperer," and a whisperer separates friends. You don't want to do that to your mate.

Early in our marriage Mack would share things with me, and I thought they were funny; so I would share them. I didn't know they were things that he just wanted me to know. He took it personally. As we've grown closer over the years, I have learned what to share and what not to share. A good principle to follow is, if you're not sure, don't say anything.

Establish a Secure Atmosphere

Security is a part of confidence. Friends will look for ways to create security in one another. "Honey, I invested in this insurance policy so if something happens to me, you and the kids will be taken care of. I'll put it right in here where all the important papers are. You are taken care of." This interprets to her, "He loves me. He really loves me."

When Brenda was growing up, her dad left home and never really came back. He was away most of the time. They couldn't even find him when their mom died. I saw a need to re-enforce security in her life. One way I do that is I never leave the yard without telling her where I am going and giving her a time when I'll return. I tell her, "Honey, I've got to go to the store and pick up (whatever) and it will take me about ten minutes." She knows, unless I have a flat tire or the car engine blows, I will be back then.

When a man tells his wife what he is doing, it comforts her. And when he says ten or fifteen minutes, he better make sure it is ten or fifteen minutes. That develops trust.

There is the same requirement for wives. Out of respect for her husband, a wife should purpose to be a woman of her word. When she tells her husband she's going shopping and she'll be back in two hours, then she should do that. Husbands and wives should always do what they say they are going to do. Trust increases confidence and security.

Unless security and confidence have been developed, fear, complaints, and murmuring will come forth.

It's important to look good, but your confidence cannot be built on looks. When we were hit by a car driven by a drunk driver, we were taken to an emergency room. Brenda was lying on the table next to me. My scalp was split. The doctor walked up to me, opened my scalp and said, "This scar goes all the way down to your skull." Then he closed it up and left. A lot of things were going through my mind, because I hadn't been able to look in the mirror. Things began to go through my mind like, "God, is my face going to be messed up the rest of my life? Will Brenda love me with this scar? Will this scar make a difference?"

Physical beauty is part of the attraction that initiates the relationship, but there has to be something about that person, on the inside, that you fall in love with. If not, your love will be so shallow it will seesaw all the time. The love has to be unconditional for the friendship to be there.

Confidence also comes with obedience and submission. When we are obedient to the commandments of God and submitted to His will, then we can go readily to the Father God and ask Him for anything.

> **Beloved, if our heart condemn us not, then have we confidence toward God. And whatsoever we ask, we receive of Him, because we keep His commandments, and do those things that are pleasing in His sight.**
> **1 John 3:21,22**

> **And this is the confidence that we have in Him, that, if we ask any thing according to His will, He heareth us: And if we know that He hear us, whatsoever we ask, we know that we have the petitions that we desired of Him.**
> **1 John 5:14,15**

If a woman has been a loving wife to her husband and has done the things that are pleasing to him, then she can go right straight to him in confidence and tell him what she wants and he will do it for her, because he is a loving husband. And the way he became a loving husband was by drawing closer to his loving Father. Both husband and wife will increase in confidence and security as they draw from the One who made them both.

From the day the husband and wife make their vows before God, they must be confident that they love one another above everything else under God.

Intimate friends hold nothing back from one another. When we first got married, I had a lot of areas I held back from my husband. Mack would say, "Are you sure you're my wife? Don't you know your body is no longer yours, it's mine?"

I'd say, "No it is not; it's still my body." And I acted like it, too. But as I began to become intimate friends with God, I began to realize that, as an individual, I was no longer my own. As sons and daughters of God, we are no longer our own. As we learn how to love the Father God, it causes us to know what to say, what to do for our intimate friend — our mate — on earth.

• Husbands: always keep your promises, quickly. Women never forget a promise made to them — never!

3
Confrontation Is Necessary

The second ingredient to developing an intimate friendship is confrontation. Proverbs 17:17 says, **A friend loveth at all times, and a brother is born for adversity.** God is telling us that we are not always going to agree with people; we are not always going to agree with our mate. But God told us what we were going to do about it before He told us about the adversity. When adversity comes, the Word of God says we are supposed to "love at all times."

All of us have confrontations: a face to face experience. You don't want a friend who will always agree with you; that is not a friend. The Word of God says, Woe unto you; be aware of men that always agree with you. (Matt. 15:8.) They didn't agree with Jesus so you know they are not going to agree with you. When you come face to face with a problem or situation, you've got to confront that. A close friend will tell you the truth even if it means losing a friend. That is the degree to which they love you. They would rather you know the truth and cast them aside as a friend than for you to lose your life.

There have been times that we have had to confront one another about something that maybe one of us didn't realize was going on. We didn't like it; nobody really wants to be confronted because it means someone disagrees with what you think, but the Bible says, **Open rebuke is better than secret love** (Prov. 27:5). Rebuke means "to reprimand sharply."

It used to be, when the telephone would ring, I thought I had to answer it. Mack would be at the point of having had all the conversation with other people that he could handle for the day. He'd say, "I'm through talking on the phone." I didn't *listen* to what he was saying. Finally he confronted me. "You don't listen to me. You don't value what I feel or think."

"Yes, I do," I said, defensively.

He said, "No, you don't. If you did, you would not have answered the phone." At that particular moment, the telephone seemed to be more important than my husband. I made the correction necessary.

If you love someone, and they are in error, then you are going to tell them, "You are missing it." We have that kind of a relationship. That's why we are able to be as strong as we are: we don't mind hurting one another's feelings if it means correcting, rebuking in love.

When correcting one another, it is usually better to use the "sandwich effect." Start by saying something good. Then tell your mate the problem or situation. Allow them to express themselves. If you come into agreement immediately, that's great. If not, conclude with "Let's just pray about it," and a kind remark concerning how good it is that the two of you can always discuss what is bothering you.

> **Faithful are the wounds of a friend; but the kisses of an enemy are deceitful.**
>
> **Proverbs 27:6**

Sometimes our friends get hurt when we tell them the truth. But after they are healed, if they ever get in trouble again, they know they can count on us.

Ointment and perfume rejoice the heart: so doth the sweetness of a man's friend by hearty counsel.

Verse 9

Iron sharpeneth iron; so a man sharpeneth the countenance of his friend.

Verse 17

When a person is welding metal, fire sparks. If you have ever been around a husband and wife, and it looked like fire was sparking everywhere, that means they are close friends! We have had those situations when sparks were flying and we thought, *Boy, if it hits the curtains it might catch the house on fire!* There have been times we even have wondered whether we married the right mate. We realize now that we did. But at the time, sparks had to fly because we were sharpening one another. Now we fit together real well, but we had some years when we had to work on it and sparks had to fly.

God has ordained that husbands and wives speak the truth to one another. But, the way men and women react to receiving that truth is quite different. When a woman tells her husband he is in error, it hits him like a slap in the face — it hurts right then — and in about five or ten minutes, if she hugs him, he's all right. But a woman does not get over it as quickly. She must be approached more slowly. If a husband corrects his wife, it generally takes her a little more time to heal — it shouldn't take days — but it will probably take more than five minutes.

God made man from the dirt; men are tough. Women were made from Adam's side. God took special time and tenderness in creating women; they need to be treated tenderly.

Wives realize they need to be confronted; they don't desire to remain in error. But husbands must know that they're not going to be ready to kiss and hug and go to bed and make love right then. No, they'll love their husbands, but it's a process for a woman's feelings to heal.

Mack, I believe, is the very best husband in the world, and I love him. I know at times he has to confront me and correct me; and when he does, I never like it. I never can see what he's saying right then. I always feel I have good reasons for doing what I did. But I respect my husband, and I've learned to listen to him. I know he loves me; I don't doubt that for a minute. But when my husband corrects me, I have to go through a healing process. The wound has to close up a little bit. He helps that wound to close by reinforcing, "I love you. I think you're the greatest wife in the world." Words of love and encouragement help to heal the wound more quickly.

Then it is the power of the Holy Spirit that helps the person to walk in that correction. And it takes time. It takes time because when you are given instructions, when you are confronted about error that you're walking in, you need time to learn another way. You are so used to doing it a certain way and now you have to either not do it or do it in another way. You've got to be led by the Holy Spirit.

It is necessary to think before you move. Sometimes this time of thinking can be misinterpreted by your spouse. Your spouse may ask, "Are you okay?" Yes, you're okay, but you have to think about what your spouse has shared and how you are going to make the changes. In times like this, Mack may ask me, "Honey, what's wrong?" I tell him, "Nothing is wrong. I'm just trying to stay in tune with God. God is dealing with me."

When we go through a time of fasting and prayer, we try to be a little more quiet, because we're meditating and leaning and inclining our ears to God. We use a time of fasting and prayer to break yokes in our personal lives, because there are some things that we are still dealing with; we haven't reached perfection here.

The devil knows you're not going to turn your back on God; you're not going to take drugs or commit adultery. But the devil will literally destroy you in your home if you don't get out of bitterness, resentment, anger, backbiting, and strife.

We have to put ourselves in a position that we can daily receive correction from our mate without responding in anger or resentment. And you have to stay close to God to do that. But if you will put yourself in that position with God, you'll see some yokes will be broken and you'll see yourself being changed from within and without.

Some people get divorced just when they are on the verge of friendship. God is getting ready to bless the relationship and they get divorced. Then they have to start all over again.

If you want to have a happy marriage, become your mate's best friend. Listen to one another. Nurture and care for each other. Every time you get together with your mate it ought to be a privilege and a joy, even if it includes a time of correction. Put a high value on the mate God has given you and watch your marriage be like heaven on earth.

• Men, when you stand before God, you will be rewarded, first, according to how well you took care of God's daughter, your wife.

4
Intimacy Grows With Counsel

The primary Scripture for this point is Psalm 1.

Blessed is the man that walketh not in the counsel of the ungodly, nor standeth in the way of sinners, nor sitteth in the seat of the scornful.

But his delight is in the law of the Lord; and in His law doth he meditate day and night.

Verses 1,2

It's very important that when we seek out counsel that we seek it from godly, upright people. Then when you seek out godly counsel, purpose in your heart to act on the counsel that you receive.

One thing we have found is that, a lot of times, people don't want to know the truth. They know they are in error and want counsel, but they will go to someone who has not been successful. For example, maybe a lady at your work is having marital problems. She knows you are very happily married. Your husband drives you to work, opens your door, escorts you into the front door and then kisses you goodbye. He sends you flowers at work for your birthday and your anniversary. She knows you are happily married because you always speak kind words about your husband. But as she is approaching divorce, she goes for counsel to someone who has already been divorced several times. She has made up her mind what she wants to do, she does not want counsel, she wants someone to agree with her. The Word of God says if you seek counsel, you should seek godly counsel.

It is possible to set yourself back five, ten, fifteen, twenty years because of the counsel you listen to and the people you associate with. If you want a happy marriage, associate with other couples that are happily married. And you can tell quickly if they're really happy or not by going home with them.

There are many people who know that we are a happily married couple because they have been in our home with us and they have seen that we don't act any differently at home than we do in church. What we live we preach, and what we preach we live.

If you are having financial problems, you should put yourself around people who have been financially successful. If you are displeased with your appearance, it's your own fault. There are people who have expertise in makeup, hairstyling, and fashion. Draw from those who have that knowledge, because it will make you a better person. Whatever you want to do in life, put yourself around people who are successful in those areas. That's part of exposing yourself to godly counsel.

Where no counsel is, the people fall; but in the multitude of counsellors there is safety.

Proverbs 11:14

Be serious about finding godly counsel. Purpose in your heart to find God's answer to your situation. Put yourself around the right people. Many times, when you receive godly counsel you are inspired; but eventually, somehow, you forget the knowledge that you gained from the one who counselled you. Keep your mind renewed by focusing on God's answer, or you will lose the direction you have been given.

Someone said people are like balloons — they leak. Any time we open our mouth we are giving out — whether it is godly counsel or not — we are giving out. When we give out, that is a leaking process. We've got to renew. We've got to put in that which we give out. Personally, that is why we try to go to conferences and seminars and put ourselves around men and women of God who are more mature in the things of God than we are. We purpose to receive inspiration from God; we purpose to receive knowledge, and then we purpose to keep it.

If you will purpose to keep the Word given to you, the devil cannot snatch it away. He will try, but he will not be successful if you keep yourself surrounded by the Word of God.

The devil will always try to show you the weaknesses of the very person who can help you the most — your mate. He constantly wars against the husband and wife. Second Corinthians 10:5 says,

> **Casting down imaginations, and every high thing that exalteth itself against the knowledge of God, and bringing into captivity every thought to the obedience of Christ.**

So when the devil comes against your mind, cast down his thoughts.

When I used to wake up, Mack would be staring in my face. I'd ask, "What are you looking at?" I was paranoid.

"I'm just admiring what God has given me," he said. He was looking and I started looking. I said, "Wow," and he said, "Wow." Then it was hard for us to get up out of the bed. You learn to appreciate one another.

Purge Past Prejudices

In 1979 God spoke to us and said, "Whatever way the devil is getting to you to keep you from being good friends, close that door."

You may be having a hard time relating to your mate because of past prejudices that are in you.

People have said to us, "I didn't even know that was in me until I got married. Then, when something went wrong, I let my mate have every prejudice I've ever had toward the opposite sex."

All of us still have some things in us that are not what you would call "good thoughts" against the opposite sex. Men frequently say, "Women just spend all your money. Boy, you'd better watch yourself. You can't ever please them." Then ladies often say, "He wants sex all the time!" You'd be amazed at how much of that is in you. You are programmed like that and you don't even know it is there until you are put into a position where you've got to show love.

Some men cannot work under female supervision because of their prejudice. The female has never done anything to them, but they just have that prejudice inside of them. There are some women who have made up their minds, because their dads were not loving dads, they will never submit themselves to any man. So they take over and run everything and put down every man. We've got to cleanse ourselves, both male and female, of things that are contrary to the Word of God.

An essential element of friendship in a relationship is respect. You've got to treat your mate as an equal. The man is not better than the woman, and the woman is not better than the man. They are different; they have different functions, but they are equal. Treat each other as equals.

Men, one of the ways to keep being a good friend to your wife is to clean up the mess that you make. Purpose to pick up your underwear, socks, and shoes. This shows respect for your friend.

A point for the ladies to keep in mind is that the men usually get dressed first so they spend quite a bit of time waiting on you. As you are patient with their efforts to be a better friend, it will help them to be more patient also.

Timing Is Critical

We are discussing developing intimacy through counsel and an important point is this: be kind and be wise in selecting the right time to consult with your mate. And if you need to make a big decision, don't make that decision by yourself without consulting your mate. If there's a decision that involves your mate, don't make the decision for them. Make the time to talk to your mate.

One afternoon three minister friends of mine were at my office. I called Brenda at about 5:30 p.m. and told her I was bringing them home for dinner. Although she was pulling her hair, she fixed the dinner. After my three friends were gone, we discussed it! I've learned to say,

"Honey, I've got three friends here and they look hungry. Could you get dressed so we can take them out?" rather than putting the pressure on her.

When you make decisions on your own, you show no consideration and no respect for your friend.

Now, we've been married for over twenty years, so when we're out shopping for each other, there are some things we know the other one would like, so we buy it.

When I go shopping for Mack, suits jump off the rack into my arms, because I know what he likes.

I like Brenda in flashy outfits, with all the shiny sequins on them. But when there's a borderline situation I'll say to the clerk, "Hold this right here. I'll be back in about two or three days, and I'll have my sweetheart with me. I'm not quite sure which one she would like. Hold them both and I'll bring her back." That way I'm sure the purchase will please her.

It is necessary to watch how you talk to one another when you need an answer in a hurry. Many couples talk to each other in passing. When you are tired and worn out is not the right time to consult your mate. Try not to have heavy topics when you just get home in the afternoon, because you have had heavy topics all day that demanded your attention. If you have to talk about something heavy, schedule a time for it. But when you schedule it, let your mate know what the topic is going to be. If we have to talk about something heavy, we'll say, "Honey, I need to talk to you about (whatever) at (whenever) time."

I used to tell Brenda I needed to talk to her and then leave her hanging. Then she would worry and start thinking, *Oh, what have I done now?* Tell your mate what the topic is going to be and then schedule a time to discuss it. This is, in general, good communication. We all make mistakes and get over in the carnal area. But don't get angry and hold it in so long that when the words come out they come out with a punch. Use some seasoning. Be careful how you talk to one another when you're in a hurry. Don't snap.

Sometimes there is no good way to "break in" to a conversation. When you are delayed because you ran into a friend or you wrecked the car by hitting a tree, there may be no good way to say it. But be careful how you say it and be careful how you respond to your mate.

Husbands, words interpret to the wife the level of friendship that you have with them. Men have a habit, because they are the ones in charge of discipline of the children, usually, to talk in a stern voice to the wife as if they were talking to children. You don't talk that way to your wife. You soften the volume, way down. Speak softly.

Sometimes, you can feel the intensity when you walk by one another; you already know things aren't all right. As the intensity builds you wonder, Should I go for it now? The Holy Ghost will say, "Keep your mouth shut." It's a good time to pray in the Holy Ghost.

The Bible says a soft answer turns away wrath. (Prov. 15:1.) Do it sometime and watch what happens.

Nabal — A Negative Example

In the first book of Samuel, chapter 25, we see where a husband's lack of sensitivity to his wife and his refusal to accept her counsel not only cost him his wife, but also his life.

Here's a husband who was very rich. Many women of the world, if you ask them what they are looking for in a husband, they'll say they want to marry a rich man. But if he's not sensitive, if he doesn't know how to minister to you emotionally, it could be the worst thing you have ever done. In this story in Samuel, this rich husband knew nothing about how to listen to the counsel of his wife.

> **And there was a man in Maon, whose possessions were in Carmel; and the man was very great, and he had three thousand sheep, and a thousand goats: and he was shearing his sheep in Carmel.**
>
> **Now the name of the man was Nabal; and the name of his wife Abigail: and she was a woman of good understanding, and of a beautiful countenance: but the man was churlish and evil in his doings.**
>
> **Verses 2,3**

David had been hiding from Saul, and he and his men were very hungry. He sent some of his men to ask this man Nabal if possibly he could send them some food. This man was so evil he said, "Who am I? Why is he asking me to do this? David could have gone ahead and taken some sheep, but he sent the men in to ask him. Abigail did not know until later how her husband had treated David.

> **And David said unto his men, Gird ye on every man his sword. And they girded on every man his sword; and David also girded on his sword: and there went up after David about four hundred men; and two hundred abode by the stuff.**

But one of the young men told Abigail, Nabal's wife, saying, Behold, David sent messengers out of the wilderness to salute our master; and he railed on them.

But the men were very good unto us, and we were not hurt, neither missed we any thing, as long as we were conversant with them, when we were in the fields.

Verses 13-15

This woman, walking in the things of God, then began to move by the Holy Spirit. If her husband would have been sensitive to the Holy Spirit and to his wife, it would have spared his life. She began to get some food and went to David. Watch her words closely.

And fell at his feet, and said, Upon me, my lord, upon me let this iniquity be: and let thine handmaid, I pray thee, speak in thine audience, and hear the words of thine handmaid.

Verse 24

David did something that her husband wouldn't do: he listened to her. A man's value appreciates when he gives a woman his undivided attention.

Then when he listens, he needs to put some action with it. It won't work to say, "I heard you," and then go do the same thing over and over because that's part of his routine.

And now this blessing which thine handmaid hath brought unto my lord, let it even be given unto the young men that follow my lord.

I pray thee, forgive the trespass of thine handmaid: for the Lord will certainly make my lord a sure house; because my lord fighteth the battles of the Lord, and evil hath not been found in thee all thy days.

> Yet a man is risen to pursue thee, and seek thy soul:
> but the soul of my lord shall be bound in the bundle of
> life with the Lord thy God.
>
> **Verses 27-29**

She begins to edify David, telling him that she knows he is God's man. When she goes back to her husband and tells him what she did, the Bible says his heart got hard. From that moment on a sickness set in on him, and in ten day's time he died. He was so evil and so harsh. Here's a man who was given counsel and understanding by his wife, but he had already made up his mind. He was so set on doing his own thing he couldn't take advantage of that counsel. He ends up losing his life, and his wife.

> And it came to pass about ten days after, that the
> Lord smote Nabal, that he died.
>
> And when David heard that Nabal was dead, he said,
> Blessed be the Lord, that hath pleaded the cause of my
> reproach from the hand of Nabal, and hath kept His
> servant from evil: for the Lord hath returned the
> wickedness of Nabal upon his own head. And David
> sent and communed with Abigail, to take her to him to
> wife.
>
> **Verses 38,39**

What's going through David's mind? This woman, not only is she beautiful, but she has tremendous understanding and she perceives how the Holy Spirit works. He proposed to her and we don't see Abigail really wasting any time. She is ready to get out of this relationship, ready to go.

> And she arose, and bowed herself on her face to the
> earth, and said, Behold, let thine handmaid be a servant
> to wash the feet of the servants of my lord.

And Abigail hasted, and arose, and rode upon an ass, with five damsels of hers that went after her; and she went after the messengers of David, and became his wife.

Verses 41,42

What made her so ready to go? David listened to her counsel. He was ready to kill; but she noticed, even in his anger, he would listen to what she had to say.

• You will succeed in your marriage and your friendship if you seek diligently the knowledge that comes from God and from couples who have a happy, solid marriage.

5
Companionship Cultivates Intimacy

When Mack wants me to spend time with him he is a jealous man. He doesn't want the television, the kids or anybody else; he just wants me. When I have things holding me back from him, deceiving me, then I have problems. God is a jealous God; when we are not spending time with Him He is jealous.

> **A man that hath friends must shew himself friendly: and there is a friend that sticketh closer than a brother.**
> **Proverbs 18:24**

The Word of God says that when you are married you are no longer two, but you have become one flesh. (Eph. 5:31.) That doesn't mean that as individuals you don't have your own individual ideas, but when it comes to anything pertaining to you as a couple, then you're supposed to blend. You're supposed to be speaking the same things, doing the same things. And that brings forth intimacy. If you never do anything together after you get married, then you can forget intimacy. Before you got married, you went to the movies, to dinner, and enjoyed spending time together.

It's a shame. There are more people who go to hotels prior to marriage than they do after they get married. We travel, and when we travel we have to stay in hotels.

It hurts our hearts when we see young couples coming out of hotels at midnight and we know they're not married. We know what's going on.

Sometimes husbands think, **I'm paying for a house. I don't need to pay for a hotel.** That's not the point. It's just the idea of getting in another environment or doing something special. Forget the money, because if you can receive that love and unity, the money is going to be there for the rent and the groceries. Maybe you had forgotten that your mate was such a good lover! Put yourselves in a neutral place, and rediscover each other.

When both partners are at home, don't be busy doing things. If the clothes aren't folded, that's all right. Often a man will spend his time working on his car; the woman will work around the house. Stop! Take time to be together. Sit beside one another and enjoy the companionship of your mate.

The reason most couples can't become intimate friends is because they're too tired. After they've struggled with the kids, gone to work, come home, fixed dinner, all they want to do is get to bed and get to sleep. They're tired. They need rest. When you're tired, sometimes your mind is cloudy. But when you rest, you can pray. As you pray, God reminds you to appreciate that gift that He has given to you. Because you love God, love that person in the flesh. When you rest, you can talk. When you talk, you won't be putting each other down. You'll be saying, "Honey, I thank God for you. You're the best thing on this earth."

When you have a friendship, you must watch what you say to your friend when you are in a hurry. Most of us get up in just enough time to wash our face, brush our teeth and go. There is no relationship here. Wake up in enough time to pray together. Don't do everything always in a rush. Women do not do well under constant pressure. If everything is always on a time limit, then she won't be fun to be around because she can't handle it. When you become friends you think ahead to what it is going to take to keep your mate happy.

We have four kids. It's really a miracle when you think about getting them all up by a certain time and getting them ready. So I know that unless I get in there and do something to help, Brenda is going to get behind schedule. I cannot be the spiritual man, sitting back praying in the Holy Ghost, while she gets everyone ready. If I want to pray in the Holy Ghost, I should get up an hour earlier.

Take careful notes of what delights your mate. The end result is that you want them happy, every day, all the time. Friends learn to love you and appreciate you when you look ugly and when you look good. On those days when the husband comes home and he's lost his job or the wife has been chewed out by her boss, and they are feeling lower than low, or they've been sick for several days, it is at those times you find out whether you have a friend. A friend will say, "I'm committed to you."

Many times the reasons we don't have friendship in our relationship is because we've cut out the action. It's amazing what healing can take place from the touch of a friend. Sometimes it is a gentle touch on the hand across the table when you are eating lunch. Sometimes it is eye to eye contact.

You really don't know a person until you go to live with them. In the hard times, in the tough times — when it seems like you are not going to get that car, when it seems like you are not going to get that dress, when it seems like you are not going to get that house — you've got to verbally express to the other one, "I love you and I'm not going to leave you." A good friend seeks to build up his friend. Build them up. Edify them. Charge them up.

We have heard many men say, "I love my wife, but I don't want to be around her." Then they don't really love her. You want to be around the one you love.

We are around one another twenty-four hours a day. We work together; we are friends together; we are husband and wife together; we are co-pastors together. Some people think they need a break from their spouse. Well, that's what's wrong with them now; they've had too many breaks.

Look at Romans 14:19.

> **Let us therefore follow after the things which make for peace, and things wherewith one may (build up or) edify another.**

The Holy Spirit is always ready to give information on how to build up your mate. Whether or not you hear it is according to your will. A stubborn, hard, stiff-necked, rebellious will ignores that communication and listens instead to the voice of selfishness. But a will that says, "Yes, Lord, I want to please You," will give in to that voice that tells how to please and edify one another.

Do you have a mate who is always critical? It is probably because you have been critical. Listen to what has been coming out your mouth. If your mate is always criticizing you, knocking you down, then go back and think about what you have been saying. Watch the situation change as you begin to speak edifying words. What you sow is what you reap.

Our words and our mouths create the atmosphere that we're going to have in our home. If we want our mate to desire to be around us, we will have to use our words to encourage and love each other.

• Be a good listener; it will help you to be a good mate.

6
Develop Intimacy
Through Commitment

Commitment means making a decision and sticking to it. Many times when couples get married, they've made elaborate plans for the wedding but when they make their vows they are just saying words and don't realize the commitment they are making.

A lot of people want to get married, but it is almost like they want to get married just for the sake of getting married. They are not thinking about the commitment involved in marriage. When you say, "I vow to live with you for the rest of my life through thick and thin, through good times and bad," that is making a lifetime commitment. But today, the divorce rate is one out of two and that is in the Body of Christ, as well as in the world.

What is happening? People are making vows and they are not taking their vows seriously. God said that if we make a vow we need to hold fast to that vow. (Eccl. 5:4,5.) God says that the man should leave his mother and father and cleave to his wife and the two should become one. (Matt. 19:5.) That word cleave means "to stick like glue." It is a lifetime commitment. Commitment is a pledge of oneself to another.

It is entrusting one's well being to another. When a young lady says she is committing herself to becoming a man's wife she is saying that she is trusting that man, not her mom and dad, to provide for her for the rest of her life. When a man makes a vow saying that he is committing to be a husband to his wife, he is committing to provide for that wife and for any children they have or bring into the relationship.

Frequently when couples get married, in one out of two cases, one of them already has children. When you go into a marriage relationship and there are children involved, then you are committing to that mate and those children.

Commitment and friendship in marriage is not on condition. It is unconditional. You have made a commitment, a decision, and you should stick to that commitment even if things don't go your way. Obviously there are going to be some good times and some bad times, some high times and some low times, but that is why people should not make the commitment unless they plan to keep it.

You may have married the wrong person, and you just could not live together. But when you meet the right person the next time, then you ought to take serious time to realize, to meditate, and think about what you are entering into so you won't make the same mistake you did before.

To become intimate, both people have to develop a relationship with God. Until they are intimate with God, sold out completely to Him and obedient to Him and His commandments and ways, they are not going to love each other as they should.

Commitment is more than just words. It is a way of life.

Mack has come dragging out of church saying, "If I can just get home and get to bed, I'll feel better." When we get home and he gets in bed, then I get in bed with him, and he sure gets healed. It never ceases to amaze me; I guess I'm good medicine!

When the wife is sick and down in the bed, that is the time a close friend — a husband — should step in and ask, "Baby, what do you feel like you can eat?" A wife needs that every now and then. She'll go as long as she can, but when she is sick and in bed, don't expect her to get up and cook and then go back to bed. Bring food in to her, and she will get well real soon.

Friendship goes beyond the physical. It goes down into the area of the emotional. When you get down inside one another, you know what one another thinks. Friendship is the doorway to intimacy. You've got to communicate on everything. God has put the man in the position of being the head, so when there comes a point in their relationship where there is not agreement, the wife needs to say, "You're the head, so you see what God says and I'm right behind you." That keeps the pressure on the man to make sure he's hearing from God.

You don't force a commitment. You don't force your mate to be something that you want them to be. God, through the Holy Spirit, will make them what He wants them to be. When Mack and I were first married, I thought he would do anything I wanted, but reality hit, and I found out that paycheck he was making didn't go very far.

At that time, I used to buy Brenda cards and write her letters. I thought that was pretty good. I didn't have it figured out yet. My letters were good, but she wanted presents too.

But I was committed to him so I wasn't going to leave him just because we didn't have everything we needed. A lifetime commitment means just that — it's for life.

If you men are going to have a good woman, you need to provide emotional security.

We're the best of friends and there is nothing we can't talk about. That doesn't mean we agree on everything, but we can talk about anything. If we come to a corner of disagreement, then we pray about it; and as we pray about it, we find out what the Father God has to say about the best way to handle that situation. It is important to realize that in some instances the Spirit of God will tell the wife, "You need to listen to your husband even though he may not be right. You need to respect him because he is your head."

God is a big enough God to handle it. If we love the Father God, then we will trust Him. If we trust Him, then we are going to obey what He tells us to do. So if He tells a wife to listen to her husband, then she will have to trust God and listen to her husband. There are times that the wife may have made the right decision, but the husband will say, "No, I don't see it that way." But as he goes to His Father God, then God will tell the husband, "You need to listen to your wife." This is a two-way street. Neither one of you is right all the time, and you've got to be able to walk with God close enough to know when the voice of authority comes through the other person.

In the spiritual realm, male and female are equal, but in the physical realm there are functions for each one. A problem in the world today is that the men are weak and the women have become rebellious. Men and women have not yielded to the Lord. But women are looking to men for leadership. They don't want to lead. Men create dominant women because the men are weak; they fail to be a friend to their wife and fail to provide for her.

A vital element in a friendship is fidelity. Inside of your mate is the ability to be the greatest lover that you will ever need, but unless you minister to them and become their friend, they will not have the desire to give themselves. God made you with a built-in desire to share your love. The secret is, we have to stick with the Bible to know how to do it, then be open to listen to our mate. We've got to communicate deep things. There's nothing that we can't talk about, but there was a process to that. Most of marriage is a process.

In friendship there has to be the freedom within the relationship to suggest new ideas because your needs continue to change over time. We've been married now almost twenty years. The basic needs are there, that we minister to one another; but there are other needs in life that we need to talk about because things have changed. We need to be able to suggest new ideas to one another.

This is the area that causes many couples to head for the divorce court: they receive all suggestions as a personal attack. You cannot be a person who easily feels rejected or you won't go far in life. Husbands and wives need to be able to be open and honest with each other. If you are going to have a strong friendship with your husband or your wife, you've got to make a quality decision that "I'm here, baby. I'm going to be here. I am going to love you. I'm not going to run off from you. I am committed to you and this thing is going to work."

• Lust looks for what it can get. Love looks for what it can give.

7

Attention Wives

In this book, we are discussing being married and friends. In order to be a good friend, a woman must fulfill her God-appointed role as a wife. God is very specific in the responsibilities He has assigned to each mate. In this chapter, Mack and I thought it would be helpful if I, as a woman, were to share some areas that we might use as a checklist for evaluating how well we, as wives, are doing our job.

Look at Ephesians 5:33.

> **Nevertheless let every one of you in particular so love his wife even as himself; and the wife see that she reverence her husband.**

The part of the verse we're going to concentrate on is **and the wife see that she reverence her husband.** This word *reverence* means "to honor, to respect, to admire." A person that you admire is a person that is going to have your attention. You'll remember the things they teach you. You'll do the things they recommend you do.

Mack and I still laugh when we see people walking down the street eating ice cream. You see, my brother, whom I admired very much, told me when I was in elementary school (he was in college) that if he ever saw me walking down the street licking on an ice cream cone he would beat me up. That was the worst thing I could do. (For some reason, it annoyed my brother to see people standing on the street corner eating ice cream from a cone.) Since I really admired my brother, anything he told me was important. There were many days I wanted some ice cream so bad, but I would think of what he had said, and I would go without the ice cream. If you admire a person, usually you will try to impress them. I remember every time my brother came home from college I tried to impress him. I think one of the reasons I excelled academically was to impress him, because he excelled, and it made him feel good when his little sister did well in school.

Think about the people you have admired. How did you treat them?

You always had encouraging words for them. You always told them how nice they looked. You tried to make up something good just so you could get on their good side. You never made rude comments to them. You wanted to impress them.

Let's start on the checklist, ladies. Remember, this is to help us be all that our Heavenly Father has created us to be.

The first question is: *Do you show more appreciation for other men than you do your husband?*

For example, I've heard a husband (actually more than one) say, "We can come in for a counseling session and the pastor can say something and she jumps, but I've been telling her the same thing for three years, and she hasn't moved." That wife is showing more respect for the pastor than she is for her husband.

Do you show more appreciation for your boss? When your boss says, "Would you get me a cup of coffee," or, "Would you mind working late today," or, "Do you mind doing this extra paperwork," do you do it graciously and tell your husband matter-of-factly about it when you get home? Could your husband be thinking, *I asked you to get just a glass of water for me and you frowned at me.*

Do you show more appreciation for your dad? When Dad comes around, are you Daddy's little girl: Daddy, what can I get for you? What do you need? Sit in the best chair in the house (which, perhaps, could be your husband's chair).

Do you admire another woman's husband more than you do your own? For example, when you ask your husband, "Did you see the dress Reverend Timberlake bought Mrs. Timberlake?" or, "Did you see the ring Mr. Jones bought Sister Jones?" it's saying to him, "You haven't come up to par."

It wasn't intentional. You didn't know that's how he perceived that. When I've made comments like that to my husband, I did not realize I was putting him down, because I believe if my husband could do it he would. The reason I didn't have a new dress or a big diamond ring was because he couldn't buy them. A man that you admire, love, and respect is going to want you to have the best. We throw heavy weights on our husband when we constantly ask for things — a bigger home, a different car, some new furniture — unless we know the money is in the bank account.

As I renewed my mind and inclined my ear to God, He would say, "If the man could do that, he would."

All these are ways that we demean our husband — sometimes not knowingly or intentionally; but we put somebody in a higher position than our husband.

Our responsibility is to come up to high standards in admiring, respecting, and appreciating our husband. When he can, he won't hesitate to buy these things. Sometimes I have to tell my husband, "Mack, I have enough." It's similar to when Moses told the children of Israel to stop bringing gifts for the making of the Tabernacle: **For the stuff they had was sufficient for all the work to make it, and too much** (Ex. 36:7). I tell Mack, "Honey, I don't need anything else. I have more than enough."

Sometimes for birthdays and Mother's Day and Christmas he'll say, "What do you want?"

I say, "I don't need anything. I really don't."

And he'll say, "But baby, I've got to get you something."

But if I didn't respect him, admire him, and appreciate him, he wouldn't even ask me what I wanted. He wouldn't even think about it. The reason I don't want for anything is he's sensitive, because I've been sensitive to him.

The second question is: *Have you belittled or criticized your husband, his abilities, or his character, his activities?*

"You play basketball all the time, and you come home stinking every day." Or, "You hang out with the boys all the time." Or, "Is that the only kind of job you can get?" To that man, that's belittling him. A wife should always build up her husband. When people ask her what her husband does, she should be proud of him and tell them he's the best at what he does, and she knows one day God is going to put him on the top.

Never belittle your husband. Be very careful of what you say in front of friends, family, and the children.

Question number three: *Have you ever had a tendency to exert pressure on him to do something until it gets done?* That is called nagging. "I asked you last week to put those curtains up and they still aren't up." Or worse still, you come home, look right at the wall, and ask, "Are the curtains up, honey?"

I used to be very guilty of this. "I'm not nagging you, but when are you going to do it? I've been asking you for the past month, and it isn't done yet. Johnny could have done it by now." And in some cases, I would go ahead and do it myself. That makes the husband feel incompetent and irresponsible.

If you keep nagging him, he will seek other people who do not constantly remind him of his shortcomings. Over the years, whenever I've asked my husband to do something, as soon as he steps in the house, he remembers what he hasn't done.

We all know what we haven't done. Nobody has to remind us; we have a conscience; we are intelligent people. So when I ask my husband to do something or he asks me to do something, we very well know what we've been asked to do. Nagging isn't going to make us *know* it any better. Comments that build up — like, "I love you" — will accomplish a lot more.

Number four: *Do you find your trivial discussions turn into arguments?* "Honey, I'd like to talk to you a little bit.

If you've got a few minutes, we need to go over the budget." And before long, the few minutes is almost an hour, and steam is blowing out of both ears and nostrils. Yes, I've been there.

Number five: *Do you ever find yourself questioning the explanations of his behavior?* I've done this. As I leave the office, my husband says, "I'll be coming right home." I drive home, but I don't see him pulling in behind me. I begin to wonder, *Where is this guy?* Two hours later he calls home saying he's going to be late at the office. My question to him is, "But you told me you were coming home. Did you have to stay at the office?" In other words, I'm asking him, "Do you have to do what you had to do?" If he didn't feel like he had to do it, he would not have called to tell me he had to do it.

I've learned that that's questioning his behavior. It's almost like you don't trust him as an adult. If I question my husband's explanation of his behavior, I'm questioning his integrity, his judgment.

Number six: *Can you think of at least three things that you have complained about in the last week, or day?* This has the same effect as nagging. It's human nature to focus in on the negative. We can have a great week and do one wrong thing, and that one thing will overshadow all the good we've done. The newspaper is filled with news, but a small percentage of it is good news; the rest is a mess. That's human nature to dig into the bad news. But we have to renew our mind and think like God thinks. God is a good God, and God brings good news. He said that we're supposed to bring glad tidings to the meek. (Isa. 61:1.) If we're His children, we're supposed to bring good news.

Number seven: *Have you ever compared your level of awareness to his?* Again, I am guilty. First Peter 3:7 says the wife is the "weaker vessel." That doesn't mean we're necessarily weak in strength; but that means we're more sensitive, more fragile. When an object like crystal or fine china is shipped through the postal service, the package is marked "Fragile. Handle with Care." The package is supposed to be handled with special care. It is not to be thrown around, because there's something in there that, if it's mistreated, could be damaged. Females are fragile; it doesn't take very much to damage them.

They are more sensitive to others' emotions than men are. At times a woman may be sensitive to something going on in another person's life, but the man may not be aware of it at all. Women are not *better* than men, and men are not *better* than women; the two are *different*. We need not put each other down because of those differences.

A woman will say, "My husband lost his job"; the first thing a female thinks is, *What can I give you?* A man thinks, *You better get out and get a job, brother.* That's just the difference.

Begin To Show Honor

We've gone over the list; we can see areas where we need to improve. This is not a one-time thing. It is our desire to please our Heavenly Father and our husband. As we consider our ways more closely, we'll begin to show honor, respect, and admiration for our husband and our relationship as friend and mate will thrive.

A real turning point in our life was when I began to seek my husband's advice and opinions on decisions. For years, I didn't care what he thought; I'd do it my own way. I had a job. He could tell me what he wanted to, but if I didn't like it, it didn't make any difference to me. (And I wondered why he never wanted to communicate with me!)

Begin to seek out his advice and opinions about everything. Ask his opinion on the dress you plan to wear for church. Whenever you go out, you represent him. Mack is very concerned about what I look like when I leave home. I am very concerned about what he looks like when he leaves home. We represent each other. We discuss what we're going to wear. He'll tell me sometimes, "No, that isn't for Sunday; that's for the week." I am to please him.

We even discuss purchases. If he says, "Go with it," we go with it. But if he says, "I don't know," we hold off. We discuss these things.

Consult with your husband if you're buying furniture or even if you're just going to move your furniture around the house or change the color scheme. He's the one who lives there with you. Ask his opinion on the color for your bedroom. If you have a color in there that he doesn't like, he's going to hate to come to the room. You don't want that; you want him to love it.

Before we come to a final decision, we both have discussed it, and we're both at peace with it.

Another way to begin to show honor to your husband is to make an effort to remember his past requests and desires and begin to fulfill them as soon as possible. Maybe ten years ago, he told you his favorite meal was fried chicken, macaroni salad, and collard greens; and you're just remembering that. As soon as you can, fix that meal for him.

Ask God for help, for His ability, to help you fulfill the desires that your husband has expressed. When you begin to fulfill those desires, he will communicate more to you.

Another way to begin to show honor and admiration for your husband is to find occasional opportunities to draw attention to your husband's positive qualities when you're with other people.

Always, when I'm with other people and a person says, "Oh, you look so nice," the first thing I say is, "My husband bought this for me." It draws attention to him and shows that he is a man who is admired, appreciated, and respected. When the kids get something and say, "Oh, Mama, thank you for buying me these school clothes," I say, "No, Daddy is the one who enabled you to get this." If we are able to achieve anything, whether it's a house or piece of furniture, I say, "My husband picked this out," or, "We picked this out together."

That attitude will make your husband feel ten feet tall inside.

Whatever is in the inside of you is going to come out, so make an effort to gain an appreciation for your husband's occupation. Try to understand how important his job and activities are to him.

I had to begin to appreciate the fact that my husband was being called into the ministry. It's our role, as a female, to help our husband to fulfill the dreams and desires and goals in his own life.

It's all right for women to have their own goals and to attempt to reach some goals that they desire. But there shouldn't be that many goals and dreams that you have, as a wife, that are going to be so different from your husband's, because you should be able to reach your goals together.

If your husband has a vision for a business, yours should be the same thing. Don't say, "I'm going to have a business, too." No, say, "We are going into business together." Maybe his desire is to have an upholstery shop, and your desire is to have a flower shop. If you help him get an upholstery shop going, you can put a little flower shop up next door. You're still in it together. It should always blend in together.

With my husband being in the ministry, the more I appreciated what he believed God was calling him to do, respected him for it, and helped him to do his best at it, the more I began to be blessed.

It's my responsibility to encourage him to be the best minister he can be. I always tell him that I'm his greatest supporter, admirer, exhorter. If someone asked me, "What are you?" I would say, "I'm his greatest follower." Because he is the husband and a pastor, he leads his sheep, and he also leads his wife. I should be the greatest follower above anybody else.

I don't care what job your husband has, you tell him, "Honey, you're the best (whatever) that company has. And when your boss comes around, your name will come up before him, and you'll be promoted, because you are such a good worker."

As you tell him that he's the best, he is going to be elevated in his own sight and begin to know that he can even be better.

You can begin to show honor to your husband by carefully considering what he says without being hasty in giving a negative reaction. I remember sometimes, when my husband would be talking, if it seemed to be coming out a little negatively, I'd get on the defense. Before he could finish, I would find myself cutting him off, trying to explain my part, my side.

But the Word says we're supposed to hear him out and then think about what has been said.

If you don't agree, pray about it, and come back together at a later time when you both can communicate about it. As I'm praying about it, especially if it's something we've disagreed on, I ask God for His mind and wisdom. Then when we get together to discuss it, I say, "I listened to what you said this morning and heard you out. I've been thinking about it and praying about it, too. I think we need to do (whatever). But if you're still strong about it, and if you think I need to change in those areas, I will do it."

If he's missed God, he'll say, "God spoke to me and told me I'm too hard on you; that that's your character."

Here's an example: he used to make me shut up. But through the years, as he communicated with God, he said, "I was wrong. I was trying to stifle the gift that God had placed within you." But even as he would say that, I changed because it made me more aware of what I said and when I said it and to whom I said it.

As we prayerfully consider our role as wife and friend, God will show us the areas that specifically apply to our husband, areas that will make us more successful in the responsibilities God has given to us, as women.

• As a wife sows patience with her husband's efforts to be a better friend, she will reap more patience from him.

8
Men, We Have a Lot To Learn

This chapter is specifically for husbands. Over the years Brenda and I have been married, I have learned that one of the biggest problems with us, as men, is we just don't know women. We know how to look at them, because we walk by sight; but after that, we know very little. We may take time with our appearance, but beyond that we know very little about how to please a woman, very little about relationships.

Somehow, we, as men in a society — especially a Western culture — are only attracted to a woman who looks good. But you can't love your wife only on the days she looks good. She washes dishes, scrubs floors, takes care of the children, and many other tasks. And she has to go to bed sometime. I don't know how Brenda manages to look so good so much of the time. But men must grow up to the level of love that is not dependent on how their wife looks.

Many men have said to me, "Pastor, I don't know why my wife acts the way she does. I come home from work. I don't commit adultery. I don't beat her. I bring my money home." As men, we think that's pretty good. In reality, it's just the cream. There is a lot more to being successful as a husband than that.

More and more, even in the Body of Christ, there are men who are almost destroyed, because they come home and their wife is gone. They say, "Pastor, I was doing all the basic things." But we have to become experts at what we are doing. I believe as you get more knowledge about women, you will be better able to meet the needs of your wife. But it takes constant study.

We husbands think things are going fine, and the wife is on her way out, because she can't take it any longer — she can't take our lack of sensitivity to her needs.

Women need to be treated like a very delicate flower. A flower needs the right amount of sunshine, nutrients, and water. But if you put too much or too little on it, that flower is history. That flower needs to be handled gently.

Dwell With Them According to Knowledge

Look at 1 Peter 3:7.

> **Likewise, ye husbands, dwell with them (wives) according to knowledge, giving honor unto the wife, as unto the weaker vessel, and as being heirs together of the grace of life; that your prayers be not hindered.**

Where are you going to get this knowledge? Are you going to get it from Dad? You better talk to Mom to see if Dad knows anything.

No. You better get it from God. Get into the Word of God and find out for yourself. Get books and tapes and learn from anointed teachers. Don't be slothful. Get into the flow of the knowledge of God and be the man He created you to be.

Men, in the natural, do not seek spiritual knowledge. They are inclined other ways. But in order to grow in Christ, a man must deny himself — deny the natural part of himself — and take on the image and likeness of Jesus. Jesus said to deny ourself daily, pick up our cross and follow Him. (Matt. 16:24.)

I loved Brenda, but I really didn't have the *knowledge* of *how* to love her.

I didn't even begin to understand how I was supposed to love my wife until I fell in love with God. God began to tell me some things that went against my masculine nature. He said, "Son, why don't you tell Me you love Me?"

There are a lot of sons who just want their dads to tell them, "I love you." And a lot of dads want their sons, even if their sons are grown, to say, "I love you, Dad." But, for some reason, we don't think it's the masculine thing to do, so we don't do it. Then that carries over, and we don't speak those words to our wife, either.

But your wife always wants to hear, "I love you." Watch her blossom and flourish with those words.

Finally, I went to God. I said, "God, I don't know *how* to love Brenda. I need Your help."

God told me, "Son, I'm so happy you came to Me. I know more about wives than anybody. Let Me take you to My romance chapter and show you how I dated and loved My wife."

I gained knowledge, and so will you. Read the following, very closely. This is God's example. The book is Ezekiel 16. Look how God talked to His wife, Israel.

> **Now when I passed by thee, and looked upon thee,**
> **behold, thy time was the time of love; and I spread My**
> **skirt over thee, and covered thy nakedness: yea, I sware**
> **unto thee, and entered into a covenant with thee, saith**
> **the Lord God, and thou becamest Mine.**
>
> **Verse 8**

Notice when God passed by, He was looking. Husbands need to start looking at their wife. Look at this romantic God we've got. When I first saw my precious Brenda, over twenty years ago, I said "No other man deserves her but me."

> **Then washed I thee with water; yea, I throughly**
> **washed away thy blood from thee, and I anointed thee**
> **with oil.**
>
> **Verse 9**

Your woman can be so anointed with the Holy Ghost if you learn how to speak the Word to her, learn how to be soft to her, that she'll go out and be a blessing to everybody. Haven't you ever seen a woman walk into a room where everybody had their head down, and her fragrance, her presence turned the light on in that room? That's the kind of woman God gave me. She can walk into a situation and things liven up — especially me.

In our early years, I was dumb. I spoke all the wrong words to Brenda. She is an excitable person, a person who is outgoing, vibrant, full of energy — all the time. I was insecure, and when you're insecure, you don't see anything good about anyone. I tried to quench some of her fine qualities. I had the wrong thinking. I didn't know how to nurture her.

> **I clothed thee also with embroidered work, and shod**
> **thee with badgers' skin, and I girded thee about with**
> **fine linen, and I covered thee with silk.**

I decked thee also with ornaments, and I put bracelets upon thy hands, and a chain on thy neck.

And I put a jewel on thy forehead and earrings in thine ears, and a beautiful crown upon thine head.

Thus wast thou decked with gold and silver; and thy raiment was of fine linen, and silk, and broidered work; thou didst eat fine flour, and honey, and oil: and thou wast exceeding beautiful, and thou didst prosper into a kingdom.

And thy renown went forth among the heathen for thy beauty: for it was perfect through My comeliness, which I had put upon thee, saith the Lord God.

Ezekiel 16:10-14

God will help you to have your wife looking and feeling like royalty. And as you speak complimentary words to her, she will feel good about herself.

When I learned how to give honor to her, she gave honor to me. If you don't enjoy this relationship-oriented situation, you're not doing too well with God either. Because God says, How can you say you love Me Whom you have not seen, when you can't even love your brothers and sisters that you see every day? (1 John 4:20.) It's through relationship that the fruits of the Spirit are developed. But we don't know how to relate to one another.

Men, did you know that when you don't know how to love your woman, you're probably going to spend a whole lot of money at the doctor's office for sicknesses and ailments that have developed because you have not met her emotional needs. She'll pull inside and sicknesses will develop. She won't want to get out of bed, wear make-up, or even fix herself up. If you don't know how to treat your wife with tenderness, patience, and understanding, she will not respond to you, favorably.

Thank God more and more knowledge is becoming available to us. We can keep on learning.

Attach High Value

First Peter 3 continues, **giving honor unto the wife, as unto the weaker vessel....** The word *honor* means to attach high value. I already know that I'll never get another wife like mine. The amazing thing to me, as I watch the Body of Christ, is that people are always talking about what "lemons" they have, what bad situations they have. I have watched that same person, whose mate thought they were a lemon, become more sensitive and understanding as their mate became sensitive and understanding toward them. Honor means to attach high value.

If you attach high value to something, you are going to find out how to keep it. Consider your automobile. A man will find out what kind of oil to use, what kind of gas works best in it, everything he needs to know to take the best care of that automobile. And yet in the area of your marriage relationship, if everything goes flat, you're in real trouble, because you haven't even begun to study what makes it work, what makes it run, so how will you know how to fix it?

I'm just now walking in some things I promised in 1970. And wives do remember what you promised. During the wedding ceremony, a man may be just going *through* the vows; a woman is *memorizing* every word spoken.

As our relationship with God increases, the value we place on our wife will increase. Let me show you a good example of this. I really put a high value on my car. It was a 1976 LTD. Brenda drove with my sister to Raleigh. She was so proud of herself because she got to Raleigh and returned with the car in one piece. (She knew how I valued that car.) The very first thing I did when she drove up to the house was look at the car and ask her, "Where's my hub cap?" I didn't even see her.

She said, "What hub cap?"

"The hub cap is missing off that car. Didn't you hear something go *ting-a-ling-a-ling* as you were driving down the road?"

"No."

Every time she took that car out, I would ask, when she returned, "Where did you park? Did you get any dents in it?" But time went by, and my relationship with God increased.

She took that same car, sometime later, and was in an accident. Although she was afraid to tell me, because she knew how much I valued the car, she called and said, "I've been in an accident in the car." To her surprise, I said, "Oh, honey, I'm so glad you are all right. I can get another car." Her value had increased.

Sometimes a man will come home from work, pick up the kids, give them kisses, and then immediately heads out to the garage or tool shed. Or maybe he's gotten into a routine of going to work, coming home, sitting down and watching television. That says to his wife that she has no value to him.

God says to put a high value on your wife, and you will demonstrate that to her by your actions.

• A man will decrease in the areas that hurt his wife as he finds out how to love God.

9

Leadership Is Your Role, Not Your Option

The Word says that My people perish for a lack of knowledge. (Hos. 4:6.) Romans 1:13 says that God would not have you ignorant. This is talking particularly about male and female relationships. God would not have you ignorant, because He holds you responsible, brethren, as the head of the household. Men boastfully say, "I am the head of this house," especially when they come to church and realize that God has set the man to be the head.

As the head of your household, men, this should be your confession: "I am the head of my house, and Jesus is my head. I will not be an ignorant brother, but I'll be knowledgeable in the Word of God. I will know how to lead, guide, love, protect, and provide for my wife and my children." Unless you, men, obtain the knowledge God has provided for you, nothing is going to go right in your home. A large responsibility rests upon the female, but a larger responsibility rests upon the male.

Men have got to be good leaders. Wives need stability and direction. But a man must have spiritual instruction in order to give direction. The head of the man is supposed to be Jesus Christ; then the man is supposed to be in the headship over his wife. Unless a man's head is Christ in everything, and the wife sees him trying to please Christ, she is not going to have a will to submit to him. There are some men who make their wives submit through fear tactics, but that is not leadership.

Today, women are packing their bags and leaving; of course, God knows the real reason behind it, and they will have to give an account for their actions. But two generations ago, women didn't get driver's licenses, didn't go out and work and lived in bondage with a no-good husband.

Men are coming home in this generation and finding that, after twenty years of marriage, their wife has packed up and left. The women of this generation have educations, driver's licenses, and trades. We get many letters from ladies who say, "I just can't take it anymore. I need a break right now. I have tried for over fifteen years to express my needs to my husband, but it hasn't made any difference."

Most women who are crying for liberation, do so because they have weak men who will not communicate with them. And until you become strong in the things of God and know what you need to do as a man, you will be weak.

Let's look at some things that are involved in leadership.

Most wives simply don't know what their husband wants to do in life, where he's going. We have to communicate where we are going.

When there is no direction there's always confusion, disorder, and rebellion. Both leader and follower must know the vision. That's why we talk about vision all the time. Then, in order to walk into the vision, you've got to set goals. We talk about our goals.

When you start setting goals, there is a period of time that it takes hard discipline to maintain the goal; but when you reach it, you're so happy that you had that discipline. Before the season begins, a serious basketball player is going to practice, and practice hard, because when it's time to get on that court in competition, it is too late. Set a goal on your mortgage, when you want to pay it off. And the Holy Spirit will get involved and help you.

Write down goals where your family can see it. I used to allow anything to come up as an excuse not to take Brenda and the kids on a vacation. I began to lose my family. So I set a goal and started telling them, "This is when we're going on vacation." They started smiling and said, "We're not going to let you forget that." And they didn't. Set goals.

It is necessary to set a time to communicate on issues of importance. I used to say, "Brenda, I need to talk to you about something," but that would cause her to get upset; because when she heard that, she would think, *What did I do wrong?* She didn't know what was going on. Ladies want to know the fine details. So now I'll say, for example, "Honey, I want to talk about goal setting on our mortgage." That takes the pressure off; she can breathe easily now and look forward to that.

Men, a good leader will invest in what he honors. Mack buys 99.9% of my clothes, because he knows how he wants me to look. And he buys more expensive clothes than what I would buy for myself.

Because I put high value on her, Brenda is a good investment. Your wife is a good investment for you.

Unless we men understand the value of our wives, we will drown the delicacy of our women.

We see so many women in fear. Their husband is in such a hurry to get home after church, they say, "Let me get out of here to the car; he's going to be mad. I've been trying to get him to church for ages. Give me the tape quick." Men, don't put her in that kind of situation.

Instead of telling my wife, "It's time to go," and interrupting her conversation, I'll walk up to Brenda and take her hand. That let's her know that I'm ready to leave, but I'm being sensitive to her desire to visit.

Yet, at the same time, ladies, be sensitive to him. Men, most of the time, are occupied with practicalities. They try to have logical reasoning in things, but they might miss the fine tuning.

Understand the balance. God put us together so we could pray and keep a balance in life.

• A woman measures a man's love by the amount of undivided time that he spends with her.

10
Submission Is an Attitude

Your best friend is your mate. A person you begin to become intimate with is going to assume a certain position in your life. That position belongs to your mate.

The main goal, in order to be successful in a marriage relationship with my mate is for me, as the wife, to love and obey my husband and then to submit to him. The word submit does not mean I become his door mat. It does mean that I yield to his authority.

Ephesians 5:22, says, **Wives, submit yourselves unto your own husbands, as unto the Lord.**

God has positional authority and spiritual authority. Spiritual authority says,

> **There is neither Jew nor Greek, there is neither bond nor free, there is neither male nor female: for ye are all one in Christ Jesus.**
>
> **Galatians 3:28**

If God has placed an anointing on your life for ministry, in that realm of spiritual anointing and authority, God has no respect of persons. People should not see you as male or female. If you love and serve God, God will cause the anointing to be on your life to the degree that people will respect you in the ministry He has called you to.

But when the woman is out from that anointing and with her husband, she is his wife. In the natural, God says that the husband is the head of the wife. Women can dislike it, disagree with it, fight against it, but if they are going to please God, they are supposed to yield to the authority of their husband. They are supposed to get their husband's permission or approval before they do anything that might affect the relationship or the household in a negative way.

This word *submission* is an attitude. Submission is an attitude that we have. Submission and obedience are two different words. The Word of God says that obedience is better than sacrifice. (1 Sam. 15:22.)

If ye be willing and obedient, ye shall eat the good of the land.

Isaiah 1:19

When you have the attitude to submit, to obey is no problem.

There are some things we're supposed to submit to but not necessarily obey. We are supposed to submit to our government, according to 1 Peter 2:13. But if our government said that we were not to praise the Lord, then, as Christians, we are not supposed to obey them. We are to submit as citizens. When we drive, we're supposed to keep the speed limit. But if the government tells us to go contrary to the Word of God, then we are not obligated to obey.

In the marriage relationship, wives are supposed to submit to their husband. If the woman's attitude toward God is right, then it will be no problem. As her attitude toward Christ is in line, as she is submitted to God, as her attitudes are in line with the Word of God, then her attitude will be in the proper perspective when it comes to her mate, also.

If she loves God, then loving her husband won't be any problem, because as she looks at him, she is going to see Jesus. God made us, and He is in us — His children — and we are in Him. When we look at our mate, we look through the eyes of Jesus rather than through the eyes of our flesh. It is our attitude that keeps us in line with the Word of God.

Being friends, there are two types of love that are involved: one is *phileo*, which is brotherly love (like Philadelphia, which is known as the city of brotherly love), and the other is *agape*. When people who have just received Jesus say, "I love the Lord," they are referring to *phileo*. They know the Lord, and they love the Lord to that degree; but they're only loving the Lord because of what He has done for them. It's superficial. The first few months and years when we come to God, our love is *phileo*, because we're just learning about Him. There is no way you can truly love, *agape*, someone you don't know. We have to grow from *phileo* to *agape*.

In our relationship with one another, when we can learn to love God, *agape* and not *phileo*, then we can learn to grow in our love for our mates from *phileo* to *agape*.

Where we get in complications is the fact that we operate in *phileo*, but we say we have *agape*. The difference is that *phileo* is loving on response. If you give me what I want, I love you. But if you disagree with me, I won't love you. If you've got something I want, and I ask you to give it to me, and you don't, then I'm not going to love you. That's *phileo*. *Phileo* is conditional.

Initially, we come to Jesus for what we can get; but as we mature, we begin to love Him for Who He is.

The disciples walked with Jesus for three and one-half years; yet, they didn't really know Him. How long have we walked with Him? How well do we know Him? The point is that we cannot know our mate until we know Jesus. We cannot love (*agape*) our mate until we love (*agape*) Jesus. Originally, our love for Jesus was superficial, based on what He did for us.

But there comes a point where we have to graduate from *phileo* to *agape*. "God, if You don't give me anything else, I'm going to love You." Of course, God has already given us everything (2 Peter 1:3), but we're talking about an attitude. Our relationship with one another is in direct parallel to our relationship with God.

If you go to God to ask for a house, a car, a job, and you don't get it, do you get an attitude problem?

"I've been paying my tithes for a week, been going to church a month, and I'm two months behind in my rent."

Why have you been going to church? Why have you been serving God? Are you serving Him because you love Him and you want to know about Jesus? Or are you after what you can get?

He'll give you some things, initially. But there's going to come a point, you're going to have to grow up. There are some things we allowed our youngest daughter, Majesty, to get away with when she was crawling and when she first started to walk and talk. And there are a few things we allow her to get away with now, but not many. Why? Because she is getting to an age where she is held accountable and responsible for her attitude. She knows better. When we call her and say, "Stop," you can see that toddler knows what we mean. She'll stop and look. Sometimes there's something she's attempted to try, but we've popped those little hands or busted that bottom, so she stops. She knows we're not playing.

When we realize that God is not playing, then we won't play with Him. When we realize that God is not playing, we won't play with our mates.

As we travel across the nation, we see women who have prayed for their husband to get saved; then, when he gets saved, she does not want to submit to the authority that God has invested in the husband. She still wants to do her own thing. That is a wrong attitude.

Look at Proverbs 18:24.

A man that hath friends must show himself friendly: and there is a friend that sticketh closer than a brother.

We place God first, He is our best friend, and we love Him; then we can love and be an intimate friend to our mate.

Jesus is that friend that sticks closer than a brother. He then gives us our best friend on earth, our mate, and He expects us to stick to one another closer than brothers.

If you are friends, there is nowhere that one goes that the other will not go. A friend sticks. If you stick, then you're stuck. If you are stuck, you are not going to separate. Problems, troubles, despair...nothing is going to separate you. Confusion, disagreement, anger ...nothing is going to separate you.

Wives, ask God, "What does my friend, my husband, need?" Sometimes God will use your husband to tell you himself what he needs. And when he tells you, take notes. Say, "Honey, tell me what you need." I ask Mack that every day. The first thing in the morning, I ask him, "What can I do for you? What would you like? Would you like juice or something to eat?"

Over the years that list has decreased. He used to require a full breakfast. Now, it's just some juice. Why? Because there are other needs taking the place of those breakfasts. There are times he says, "I'd like to have some good old grits and eggs and bacon," and I say, "Okay, I'll fix it."

Then there are times later on, as we have opportunity late at night, Brenda will say, "Tell me what you want out of life. Where do you see me fit in your life?" We had problems in that area because I saw her in one role and she saw herself in another role. We were going in opposite directions, and it was causing gaps in our relationship.

We had to come back together.

As the wife, I had to say, "Mack, how do you see me fitting in our relationship?" He told me. I agreed. I'm still trying to adjust. It's a daily adjustment. Your roles change so much. You are still the same people, but the demands on your lives change every day. That's why we have to check in not only with our Heavenly Father but with one another, daily. If you don't, you're going to have concerns and cares that you need not have.

As I ask Mack, daily, "Where do you see me fitting in?" he tells me. There may be times he wants something done right then. She might say, "I can't do it right now, unless it's something that must be done immediately." There are those times, and I, as a wife, can adjust instantly. I say, "Okay, if that's what you need me to do, that's what I'll do."

Why? Because I am a submitted woman.

You women who are reading this book, I encourage you to say, "I submit to You, God. I yield to You, God. And I love You, God. Therefore, I will have no problem yielding and submitting and loving my husband."

• A relationship begins to flourish where peace and happiness abound.

11
Sensitivity Is Essential in Friendship

As friends, we need to become more sensitive to the emotional needs and desires of our mate. One of the greatest complaints, both of women and men, is the lack of sensitivity to one another's needs.

When a couple first dates or gets married, there's nothing they can't talk about. After a while, many women complain that their husband stays to himself. He never wants to talk to her. If a man is married, he didn't want to be by himself or else he would not have gotten married.

If she sees him gravitating to himself — other than him getting away to be with the Lord — something is wrong. If she will pray and ask for wisdom, God will help her to find out what is wrong with the relationship. As she sows seeds of love, God will cause the avenue to open up so she can find out what he is dealing with. Whatever is in him that is not right will come to the surface.

Men do want to talk about what is on their mind and their heart, their deepest thoughts and desires, if their wife will be a friend, if she will listen.

There are many simple things that a woman desires that a man simply misses. Wives complain, "My husband is not sensitive to me."

Perhaps the husband will respond, "I just bought her a new bedroom suite, a new living room set." And they are looking at the bigness of their purchase. But many times, it's the little things that women need.

If you talk with women who have more wealth than they could spend, and their husband buys them cars, rings, clothes, and anything else they want, they still may not be happy, because there are some very small needs that are not being met.

The things a woman calls a simple thing is often something a man misses altogether. Take for instance, there are times when a woman just needs for her husband to hug her, without any expectations. But frequently, when the wife approaches her husband, the next thing he's thinking about is sex. All that woman wants is to be embraced.

Early in our marriage, Mack was one of those embracers who liked to hug and kiss and carry on from there. At times, all I wanted was for him to hold me and hug me. That was it; nothing else. Sometimes, it caused disappointment for him because it stopped there.

Over the years, God has given us some points that have helped us to become more sensitive to the needs of our friend, our mate. It all starts with sowing seeds of love.

One desire I have had is to go fishing; but Brenda said, "I tried that one time with my brother, and I'm not going again. All you do is sit out there on the bay and throw worms in the water. I can't do that."

When we got married we said,

Wither thou goest, I will go; and where thou lodgest, I will lodge: thy people shall be my people, and thy God my God.

Ruth 1:16

But my wife decided to sow a seed of love, to show sensitivity to my needs. She said, "I want to be with you. I don't care where it is — fishing, skiing, hiking — wherever you go, that's where I'll go. If you want to go fishing, I will go with you, and we're going to catch some fish...if we fish." (When you go fishing, there's no telling what you might catch!)

But sometimes we miss our blessings, because we are too closed-minded. We want to do what we want to do and nothing else. Over the years, Mack told me, "One day, I'd like to go to a log cabin, kind of rough it." I told him, "That is definitely not for me. I like hotels." But as I listened to God, I learned to appreciate my husband, and now I listen to him. We're planning one day to either own or be able to visit a log cabin, frequently, where we can be together for a time of relaxation. He can build a fire, and we can sit back and enjoy one another.

We're talking about sowing seeds of love. Sowing seeds of love is more than sex. There are things you've got to do before you can have good sex. Sex is more than an act. It's more than the physical. It's the little things that husbands and wives do for each other to meet the needs of their mate.

Men like things like football, baseball, boxing. I remember when my wife first got into boxing. She did it only because she loved me. It was a championship match. I said, "Honey, this guy knocks them out in the first two rounds." And that was true, in every fight but that one. It went the whole fifteen rounds. But she was so sweet.

On the other hand, my time and my growth had to come when it came to shopping. I have a wife and three daughters. Men, have you ever gone shopping with four ladies? You will find out if you are developed in the fruits of the Spirit. Get used to this: walking down the mall, being torn apart. But also know on the other end that your wife will be aware of your sensitivity, and she will reward you in ways you never dreamed.

Gifts Are for Giving

There is ignorance on the part of both husband and wife in the area of giving gifts. Usually the problem is, again, a lack of knowledge. There are differences. The question is, *How can we bridge these differences?*

Most of the time, one partner will be more sensitive to what needs to be done than the other. It will seem to you, in the natural, that you're the only one that is changing. And there is no consideration on the other one's part — no thank you, no sensitivity.

But don't forget the God factor. The God factor is that God has seen your faith. He is going to begin to bless you in ways you never dreamed. Some men have told us, "I've bought my wife more dresses in the last three months than I've bought her in any one year, but yet, I've seen no change in her." Even though blessings may not be coming from her, maybe she has her eye on another dress and another dress and shows no sensitivity. God will bless the work of their hands, if they don't get over into bitterness. God sees their heart and when their motive is to make their wife happy, God will find ways to bless them. Perhaps, there will come more work for them than they expected. Another opportunity will open up. An idea will come that will bring an increase.

Whether it's the wife doing something, and she feels like the husband is not sensitive, or the husband doesn't feel his wife is sensitive, if they'll keep their prayer life with God intact, they'll reap a harvest.

God will show you, day by day, what to do. You have to walk with God daily to hear what He has to say for that day. Today He may say, "Flowers." Tomorrow, He may say, "Pick up that vase that she's wanted to match that set of candlesticks on the fireplace." Being sensitive to God will get you a long way, and nothing can take the place of that. How do you know when to do what? When God tells you.

You may be thinking, *But it's not our anniversary or birthday or any holiday.* It doesn't have to be. If God only gave us things on particular dates, we'd be in bad shape. But He rewards us as we're faithful to Him. Be sensitive to Him.

I remember years ago, Mack did not know to give gifts to me; but I would give gifts to him. I began to think, *He never gives me anything. Why do I want to give him something? I always give. In fact, I gave the last gift, and he still gave me only a card.*

Mack would take out time to buy cards, and you could tell he took time finding them because they said just the right words. Then he would write even more words on it. It was wonderful. But after I read the card, I needed more. I'd read the card and then a voice would say, "Where's the gift? This man is always giving you these cards, but where are the gifts?" The devil would tell me that Mack didn't love me, because if he did, he would give me gifts, too. But he had never been taught to give gifts.

I began to think, *What's wrong with this guy?* To him he thought he was doing something very great. And I was thinking, *I need much more.* And he says, "What more do you need? A lot of women don't even have that." But the wife is thinking, *I need more.* The man is thinking, *How much more? When does this stop? When is enough, enough?*

A husband may ask his wife, "When do you ever get satisfied? The more I do, the more you want me to do. I bought you a house, and you wanted a living room suite. I bought you the living room suite, and you wanted new kitchen appliances. If it isn't one thing, it's another."

But it's amazing, on the other side, the wife may say, "You got the car; then, you wanted new tires on the car when you got it. Then you needed new hub caps, because the ones you had were not the style for your new car. Why didn't you buy all of that when you bought the car?"

See, neither one is sympathetic to the other one's needs. But when you get *self* out of the way, you can focus on what the other person needs.

Mack had never been taught how to give gifts, so he was ignorant in that area. So, the Holy Spirit began to tell me, "Continue to give gifts to him." I would buy him gifts. I would take my last penny and give him something. One time I took my whole income tax return, about $120.00 and spent it all on him. The Holy Spirit reminded me of the Scripture that says to do unto others as you would have others do unto you (Matt. 7:12); so I bought him real nice presents.

The Holy Spirit began to speak to Mack about giving me gifts. Over a period of months, he would remember the gifts that he received throughout the year, and he began to give me gifts. Mack began to buy things for me and really not know why except he had been nudged by God to demonstrate his love for me.

I made a mistake that I want to caution you —men, as well as women — not to make. I knew how to give, but I did not know how to receive. When he bought me something I didn't like, I'd make comments like, "They must have seen you coming. Where did you get this?" When he bought my engagement ring, I wondered if it were truly an engagement ring because I could hardly see the diamond...and I asked him..."Where is the diamond?" He bought me a watch; it was silver. I said, "Don't you know you don't buy a silver watch to go with a gold ring?"

And I made the mistake too many times of taking back what he bought for me and getting something I picked out, something I wanted.

So as the Holy Spirit was working on my behalf, I was pulling out those seeds of love I had sown through giving, by putting his gifts down with my mouth and my actions. For a while Mack decided, "It will be many moons before I get you anything else." I had hurt my friend. Don't do that. Be appreciative of whatever he buys you. Thank him for the gift and for the effort he put forth.

Men, you are supposed to be the one who knows your wife better than anybody else. You are her best friend. When you are going to give a gift to your wife, *you* give the gift. You pick it out, even if you think you don't know how. It doesn't matter if it's the wrong size or the wrong color. You pick it out yourself, because there is a greater amount of love and joy in receiving it when she knows that you bought it for her. If she found out that your daughter, sister, secretary or friend picked it out, then you would have some problems.

Sow Seeds of Love

Ephesians 6:8,

> **Knowing that whatsoever good thing any man doeth, the same shall he receive of the Lord, whether he be bond or free.**

and, Matthew 7:12,

> **Therefore all things whatsoever ye would that men should do to you, do ye even so to them: for this is the law and the prophets.**

basically say the same thing.

This is regardless if you're saved or not — whatever seed you sow. If you are not satisfied about how you are being treated, then you need to begin to do good things, because God will see that those good things are done unto you. When you start giving out, then He will see to it that you are given to. It's simple: treat others the same way you want to be treated.

What better place to sow your seed than in the life of your partner? Plant good seeds to your spouse and your spouse will give good seeds back. It might not happen today, but it's going to happen.

Over the years as we have planted seeds in each other's life, our mate continually plants seeds back into our life. We are blessed. Why? Because we began to sow seeds of love.

> **Be not deceived: God is not mocked: for whatsoever a man soweth, that shall he also reap.**
>
> **Galatians 6:7**

We're discussing sowing seeds of love. Not too long ago, somebody gave us a large watermelon: it weighed about thirty pounds. It was so good, we decided to save the seeds from this watermelon so we could plant them and have more. If you've got something that's good, you want more of it. We took all the seeds and dried them out and put them in a little jar and saved them. Then we planted those seeds, and now we're looking forward to another big watermelon; because we planted the seeds. Life is the same way.

If you sow seeds of love, love is going to come back to you. Galatians 6:7 says, **Whatsoever a man soweth that shall he also reap.** If we plant watermelons, we're going to get watermelons. If we plant hatred, we're going to reap hatred. If we plant love, we're going to reap love. If you plant a little love, you're going to reap a little love. But if you plant abundant love, you're going to reap abundant love.

When we were in college, we were the best of friends. We used to go everywhere. We were such friends that people thought we were brother and sister. Then we started holding hands. Our relationship was so different from most of the other young couples: we were friends.

The coach told us, "As long as you're friends, you can stay in love." But you can be married and not be in love because you're not friends anymore. It's love that keeps the bond of friendship between a husband and wife. It works both ways.

We have noticed through the things that have happened over the years of our marriage, that as long as we can remain friends, we have no problems in our marriage relationship.

The Word of God says we have to daily take up the cross and deny ourselves. (Luke 9:23.) We're to daily die to the flesh. When we do that, then we're able to sow seeds of love to our mates.

Some people say, "It's a challenge to sow seeds to our mate, because we live with them all the time." But remember, your mate is also your best friend. If you begin to think about it like that, you will realize if you begin to plant seeds with that person you live with you'll reap a more lasting reward. It will make life so much better. You'll be able to leave home happy, and you'll be able to go back home happy. Doesn't it make more sense to sow those seeds of love into the life of your best friend, your mate?

God knew it was a challenge. That's why He said, "How can you say you love Me, when you can't love those around you?" (1 John 4:20.)

You may say, "You don't know my spouse." But we know God. And we know that when you put certain principles into focus that God's Word will not return unto Him void. (Isa. 55:11.) We must learn to sow seeds of love.

When a mother holds her baby in her arms, there is comfort that comes to that baby. Comfort comes to a husband and wife as they embrace each other. Many times you just need to come to one another and embrace one another, hug one another, say kind things to one another. There is life and death in the power of your tongue. (Prov. 18:21.)

So why not speak life? Your tongue can create any kind of atmosphere you want. It can create a positive atmosphere, an accelerated atmosphere, a motivated atmosphere, or a negative atmosphere. You choose which atmosphere. You've got to choose to do it God's way.

In order to sow seeds of love, we have to have a better understanding of what God is talking about when He says, "love." Look at 1 Corinthians 13.

Charity (that's love) suffereth long, and is kind; charity envieth not; charity vaunteth not itself, is not puffed up,

Doth not behave itself unseemly, seeketh not her own, is not easily provoked, thinketh no evil;

Rejoiceth not in iniquity, but rejoiceth in the truth;

Beareth all things, believeth all things, hopeth all things, endureth all things.

Charity never faileth....

Verses 4-8

Sometimes we allow the devil to get to us, and we are very hard toward one another. Love is kind. God is love. (1 John 4:8.) We are the children of God; we are to be imitators of God. And God is the same yesterday, today, and forever. (Heb. 13:8.)

Now, watch this. Concerning life, itself, the writer of Proverbs 4 says,

> **Get wisdom, get understanding: forget it not; neither decline from the words of my mouth.**
>
> **Forsake her not, and she shall preserve thee: love her, and she shall keep thee.**
>
> **Wisdom is the principal thing; therefore get wisdom: and with all thy getting get understanding.**
>
> **Exalt her, and she shall promote thee: she shall bring thee to honour, when thou dost embrace her.**
>
> **She shall give to thine head an ornament of grace: a crown of glory shall she deliver to thee.**
>
> **Verses 5-9**

Wisdom is the principal thing, therefore get wisdom. Get it. If you were walking along and there was a $10 bill laying there, would you walk on by and say, "I don't think I want that"? No. You would reach down and pick it up. Wisdom is the principal thing. Get it. And with all you're getting, get knowledge. When you get both of them, then you've got something going on.

When it comes down to relationships, very few people operate in wisdom and understanding. Most people have never even seen a relationship that is ruled by the wisdom and understanding of God.

The Word of God is the wisdom of God. You have put yourself in the position to get God's wisdom on how to sow seeds of love. Now, don't forget it. Keep renewing yourself, reminding yourself. Keep *doing* it.

• When you make decisions on your own, you show no consideration for your friend.

12
Understand the Difference

As male and female sometimes we hurt one another unintentionally, but — unintentional or not — the hurt is there.

In order to stop hurting each other, we are going to have to start listening to one another. We are different; maybe there will be times when we get angry with each other; but before we start thinking how dumb, how foolish the other person is, let's remember: we are different and we look at things differently.

A man needs to know things that affect a woman in the emotional realm, so he can meet her emotional needs. A woman must know how a man looks at things, so she can minister to his needs. Men usually think from a rational perspective, and women usually receive from an emotional realm. As we grow in God, there's a balance that comes.

Men are achievement-oriented. A family vacation has the potential to be a wonderful time of relaxation and fellowship or a time of continuous conflict. When the man gets in the car, he determines the number of miles that must be driven in that day in order to arrive at the specified destination. To the man, he has set a goal. He puts the pedal to the metal and doesn't want to stop.

But, there are other people in the car. The children, in a very few miles, need to stop to go to the bathroom. While the man is contemplating how this will affect his schedule, the wife enters the restroom and runs into a friend she hasn't seen in years. Of course, she will stop and visit. He still doesn't abandon his goal. Further along, there are interesting shops, sights, restaurants...anything you can think of that draws the attention of the passengers in the car. Stop. Stop. Stop.

The man's goal is now unattainable. He seems grouchy. Why? This is supposed to be a vacation. A man is so goal-oriented that it is difficult for him to see himself succeeding if he does not reach the goal he sets.

A man needs respect. There may be times when a man has had a rough day at work because the people around him didn't show him respect, or, he may feel that the job he does is not worthy of respect. Maybe he didn't achieve the goals he set out for the day. Whatever happened, when he comes home, he is feeling low.

But in his home, he is the king. He should be treated with respect as king of the house and as head of the family. Most secular material today has a very antichrist spirit in that it puts the man down. We've got to stay away from that, so it won't get in our mind. Men and women of God are very special.

That husband may look big and muscular and think he is the greatest lover in the world, but he really needs your hand softly on his back and your words quietly encouraging him, "Darling, I have faith in you, because I'm carrying your name. You're going to make it. You are my man, my king, my provider."

Conversely, a woman's feeling of success and well-being can be affected by a number of emotional factors. How does a husband meet the emotional needs of his wife? First of all, he has to identify them.

Low self-esteem. Husbands have to learn to recognize when their wife is down. Maybe she has been on the job, overworked and not appreciated. Her boss might have a rough marriage, so he takes it out on her. She may have to deal with sexual harassment. Her boss could be a woman who is unsuccessful in relationships so she's jealous and pours on extra work. She worked very hard, and nobody told her thank you for anything. Whatever the reason, when she comes home, with low self-esteem, she needs her husband to be sensitive and build her up.

Men, in this connection, always ask God to give you a way eventually, somewhere along the way, that you can bring your wife home to stay, if she wants to.

Men, you have to help her feel good about herself. She wants to look perfect. When she dresses up, you better be the first one to say, "Oh, you look good." If I don't remember to tell Brenda how great she looks, she will say, "I don't know how I look." She wants a response from me. It is not a hard thing. There is no reason to be dumb and keep our mouth shut. Let's say, "Good gracious alive, honey, you look good!"

If you don't learn how to say that, she'll go with somebody who does know. She'll find somebody who knows how to say it. It may be over lunch at work; it may be when she gets out of the car, but she needs to hear it from someone.

There are so many good-looking people in the world. It counts a lot, but it's not the highest point on the scale. Women are looking for someone who knows how to care. He could look like a bear, but if he knows how to care, how to talk, how to listen, a woman will be drawn to him.

This is something men have to learn: a woman is turned on by soft words. If you help your wife feel good about herself, she will have a smile on her face every time she is around you. She is a part of you.

In Genesis 29, God gives an example of a man, Jacob, who had two wives, and they both had low self-esteem. Jacob's father, Isaac, sent him to the house of his Uncle Laban, to marry one of his cousins. Laban had two daughters: Leah and Rachel.

> **And Laban had two daughters: the name of the elder was Leah, and the name of the younger was Rachel.**
>
> **Leah was tender eyed; but Rachel was beautiful and well favored.**
>
> **And Jacob loved Rachel; and said, I will serve thee seven years for Rachel thy younger daughter.**
>
> **Verses 16-18**

Jacob loved Rachel and wanted her for his wife. He worked for seven years for Laban to pay to marry Rachel. But Laban tricked Jacob on the wedding night.

> **So Laban invited all the men of the settlement to celebrate with Jacob at a big party.**
>
> **Afterwards, that night, when it was dark, Laban took Leah to Jacob, and he slept with her.**
>
> **(And Laban gave to Leah a servant girl, Zilpah, to be her maid.)**
>
> **But in the morning — it was Leah!**

> "What sort of trick is this?" Jacob raged at Laban. "I
> worked for seven years for Rachel. What do you mean by
> this trickery?"
>
> > Verses 22-25 TLB

The Bible says Leah was "weak eyed," which means she had no spark; she was unattractive.

Men, that may be your woman, but we don't believe there is a woman alive who cannot be attractive in a lot of ways, physically as well as spiritually. You need to find the right person to help her with her hairstyle or makeup or help her select clothes that accentuate her good physical qualities.

Jacob was not satisfied with Leah, so Laban promised him Rachel, too.

> "It's not our custom to marry off a younger daughter
> ahead of her sister," Laban replied smoothly.
>
> "Wait unto the bridal week is over and you can have
> Rachel too — if you promise to work for me another
> seven years!"
>
> So Jacob agreed to work seven more years. Then
> Laban gave him Rachel, too.
>
> And Laban gave to Rachel a servant girl, Bilhah, to be
> her maid.
>
> So Jacob slept with Rachel, too, and he loved her
> more than Leah, and stayed and worked the additional
> seven years.
>
> But because Jacob was slighting Leah, Jehovah let
> her have a child, while Rachel was barren.
>
> > Verses 26-31 TLB

Both women had a self-image problem. Although Leah was not pretty, and she knew Jacob did not love her, she was fertile and could give him children. But she noticed that many times Jacob did not come to her tent.

Jacob went into Rachel's tent, but she was unable to give him children. So they both had a problem.

And both of them had housemaids, too. The rivalry came to the point that each sent Jacob into her maid; and since the maid was property, the child that would be conceived would belong to the mistress. Four different women bore children to Jacob. But Jacob was unable to make even one wife feel good about herself. Both of his wives had low self-esteem.

Husbands need to be sensitive to their wife's self-image. Perhaps, you notice she is getting overweight. That's not the time to complain about the shocks in your car!" No. No. She didn't get like that overnight. You've watched her grow like that. You may have to start getting up earlier, exercising together, and setting a goal. We found out, in exercise, it's so much easier when you have someone to exercise with. It would be better, if you notice she is gaining weight, tell her then and begin, immediately, to exercise with her.

In Israel, in the Bible days, it was a shame to a woman if she did not bare a son for her husband. First Samuel 1 tells the story of a woman Hannah, who had low self-esteem because she had no children. Her husband, Elkanah had another wife, Peninnah, who had borne him children. Peninnah would taunt Hannah because Hannah had no children. Every year when they went to the house of the Lord, Elkanah gave portions to Peninnah and all her children, but he gave a double portion to Hannah, because he loved her. But Hannah was upset by the comments of his other wife and she cried and did not eat. Watch this wise husband:

> **Then said Elkanah her husband to her, Hannah, why**
> **weepest thou? and why eatest thou not? and why is thy**
> **heart grieved? am not I better to thee than ten sons?**
> **Verse 8**

This man, Elkanah, had knowledge of how to cheer up his wife; something that Jacob did not have. This man had so much knowledge of how to make his wife happy that he could honestly say, "I'm better to you than if you had ten sons to go get things for you."

Loneliness. One of the biggest complaints of wives today is that they're lonely. It is a puzzle to most men. But sometimes a woman wants someone to talk to. The average woman speaks about 25,000 words a day. The man speaks about 12,500 a day, and he gets them all out at work. The only thing he has to say at home is "Uh huh. Yeah."

Then he wonders, *How could she be lonely? I come home every night.* But what does he do when he gets home? Does he spend all his time watching those big, rough football players wallow in the mud over some pigskin or does he spend his time hugging his wife?

Sports are great! But none of those dudes are going to come to your house and cook your dinner. None of them can meet your needs like your wife can. When your wife says, "Honey, I'm ready to go," or "I need to talk," push that button and turn off that game. Tell her, "I'm ready to listen."

She doesn't want to compete with the newspaper or the television. She needs to know that you are listening to her. In fact, in case you haven't discovered this, women become intimate with people who listen to them. If you're busy doing something...fixing the refrigeration...and she is trying to tell you she needs a pair of shoes, you're losing ground.

If you're not sensitive to her emotional needs, she is not going to be sensitive to your physical needs. When you go into the bedroom that night, nothing is going to happen. Nothing. She was trying to tell you a problem that was important to her, but you were insensitive.

When our cat Jody ran off, I was so happy, I wanted to jump; but Brenda was upset, because that was her buddy. While I was on the road traveling throughout all of North Carolina and two counties in Virginia, Jody was her partner. The cat spent more time with her than I did. A dog took out after our cat, and the cat ran away. Brenda was so upset; she kept crying. She couldn't get over it.

We left to go on vacation. I said, "What's wrong? Are you still upset about that cat?"

"Yes. Can we call back this evening to see if he came back home?" she asked.

And still I said, "Lord, don't let him come." That's the difference. No sensitivity. We're totally different.

Absence of romantic love. When we say "love" men automatically think of *making* love. Ladies need to be loved *romantically*. The Holy Ghost can teach you how to be romantic. You may be sitting there at work and the Holy Ghost will say, "Stop by and get some flowers for her today."

You may be tempted to point out that it isn't a birthday, anniversary, or any special day. The Holy

Ghost will say, "That's right. That's all the more reason you ought to do it today."

The Holy Ghost taught me this principle. I tell men all over, don't wait for the birthday, don't even wait for the anniversary. Start getting things two or three days ahead of time. After I found out how Brenda treated me when I brought her gifts on those special days, I decided I'm foolish to wait until that day. I get a head start.

I also found that it was romantic and comforting to walk with Brenda in the malls.

At first a man may say, "No, I don't want to go there." But I found it was so romantic to walk with her in the mall, just being with her. She knows the only reason I walk around that mall is so I can be with her. She appreciates my effort and rewards me greatly.

Pressure. Always being under pressure will wear a woman down. It can cause depression, too. Read the story of the woman in Proverbs 31 who accomplishes so much. Read it closely: she had a housemaid. That's how she could do all of that.

Children can wear women out, because women operate in grace. They keep letting the kids get by. But men usually are firm. They say it and the kids do it.

Financial difficulties. Financial difficulties affect a woman much deeper than it does a man. A man is goal-oriented. He's got his eyes on the goal. He sees himself coming up out of the difficulty. The woman says, "When? I heard you say that twelve months ago." It affects a woman much deeper.

Women tend to function in security: the security that comes when provision is there. They know God is the source, but a man is asking for trouble unless he provides financial security for his wife.

The story of Rebekah from Genesis 24 is an example of the importance of security to a woman. Abraham was old and he called his oldest and most faithful servant to him.

> **And I will make thee swear by the Lord, the God of heaven, and the God of the earth, that thou shalt not take a wife unto my son of the daughters of the Canaanites, among whom I dwell:**
>
> **But thou shalt go unto my country, and to my kindred, and take a wife unto my son Isaac.**
>
> **Verses 3,4**

He told his faithful servant to go to his relatives and find a wife for Isaac and bring her back. The servant prayed for God to help him find the woman who would make his master Abraham's son happy, a woman who would serve the Lord. Specifically he said,

> **And let it come to pass, that the damsel to whom I shall say, Let down thy pitcher, I pray thee, that I may drink; and she shall say, Drink, and I will give thy camels drink also: let the same be she that Thou hast appointed for Thy servant Isaac; and thereby shall I know that Thou hast showed kindness unto my master.**
>
> **Verse 14**

He just finished his prayer when Rebekah came to the well. She gave him a drink and then drew water for his camels. She was **very fair to look upon, a virgin, neither had any man known her** (Gen. 24:16).

> **And the man wondering at her held his peace, to wit whether the Lord had made his journey prosperous or not.**

And it came to pass, as the camels had done drinking, that the man took a golden earring of half a shekel weight, and two bracelets for her hands of ten shekels weight of gold;

And said, Whose daughter art thou? tell me, I pray thee: is there room in thy father's house for us to lodge in?

Verses 21-23

She answered his questions, assured him there was room in her father's house for them, and ran to tell her family what had happened.

And Rebekah had a brother, and his name was Laban: and Laban ran out unto the man, unto the well.

And it came to pass, when he saw the earring and bracelets upon his sister's hands, and when he heard the words of Rebekah his sister, saying, Thus spake the man unto me; that he came unto the man; and, behold, he stood by the camels at the well.

And he said, Come in, thou blessed of the Lord; wherefore standest thou without? for I have prepared the house, and room for the camels.

Verses 29-31

You have to have a pretty big house to invite people in, but you have to have an extra big place to put camels. Rebekah, obviously, lived very comfortably with her brother, Laban.

The servant began to tell them of his errand.

And the Lord hath blessed my master greatly; and he is become great: and He hath given him flocks, and herds, and silver, and gold, and menservants, and maidservants, and camels, and asses.

And Sarah my master's wife bare a son to my master when she was old: and unto him hath he given all that he hath.

Verses 35,36

111

He proceeded to tell them the entire story of how the Lord had directed him in his errand. He then asked her father and brother if Rebekah could go with him.

> **Then Laban and Bethuel answered and said, The thing proceedeth from the Lord; we cannot speak unto thee bad or good.**
>
> **Behold, Rebekah is before thee, take her, and go, and let her be thy master's son's wife, as the Lord hath spoken.**
>
> **Verses 50,51**

The servant then brought out gifts for her and her family. (It's always good to bless her family.)

> **And the servant brought forth jewels of silver, and jewels of gold, and raiment, and gave them to Rebekah: he gave also to her brother and to her mother precious things.**
>
> **Verse 53**

They had a celebration that night and, in the morning, the servant asked if he could take Rebekah and return to his master. Rebekah's mother and brother wanted her to stay for a few days to prepare, but they agreed to allow Rebekah to make the decision.

> **And they called Rebekah, and said unto her, Wilt thou go with this man? And she said, I will go.**
>
> **Verse 58**

She hadn't seen Isaac yet, but she knew he was very wealthy and could provide well for her. She was eager to go.

There is a lesson in this: it doesn't matter where a woman comes from, what nationality she is, she is looking for security. She expects her husband to provide for her.

Menstrual problems. Some women may react totally different during that time. They affect some women emotionally. For some ladies, they suffer pain and discomfort during their cycle. Ladies, don't put up with that. That's the curse, and you are redeemed. You are under a new covenant. Take the Word of God and stand against the curse. (Gal. 3:13.) But husbands, this is not the time to be super spiritual and tell her, "Believe God." Show some sensitivity here.

Problems with the children. Don't ever be fooled husbands, when your wife says, "I'm not going to worry about Johnny," you can translate it, that she already is worried about Johnny. You need to know how to minister comfort to her.

There is a stage when your daughters grow past being a little girl and they make up their own mind about their hairstyles. That's the time for Dad to step in because it will affect your wife. When the little girls want to wear makeup, and the mama says yes but she really means no, Dad needs to step in.

When a woman is having difficulty with the children, it can affect her relationship with everyone. If the kids are disobedient and they talk back to Mama, trying to stand their ground and justify themselves, a wise man will quickly go in and stand beside his wife. If she gets emotionally upset, she's not going to be able to minister to his needs.

Sexual problems. You have to be knowledgeable in the area of sex. You may say, "I know how to make love." Have you asked your partner yet? Maybe you don't. And maybe they haven't been telling you. You need to find out what they want, what meets their needs.

Basically, sex in marriage gives life to both partners. Look at Proverbs 5:15-19.

> **Drink waters out of thine own cistern, and running waters out of thine own well.**
>
> **Let thy fountains be dispersed abroad, and rivers of waters in the streets.**
>
> **Let them be only thine own, and not strangers' with thee.**
>
> **Let thy fountain be blessed: and rejoice with the wife of thy youth.**
>
> **Let her be as the loving hind and pleasant roe; let her breasts satisfy thee at all times; and be thou ravished always with her love.**

Some of you reading this book, may be in the same place I was years ago: I had a mental block when it came to sex. I did not look forward to being "ravished." I didn't even want Mack to look at me. I was ashamed of my body. When we'd get in bed, I would pull the quilts and blankets up to my neck. He would come in and say, "Let me see you." I thought he might not like what he saw. But I found out, as imperfect as my body is, God has given him a love for this body.

You can get rid of that mental block by speaking and acting in faith. Begin now to say, "I'm going to learn to enjoy sex, because the Word of God says that our bodies are not our own and the marriage bed is honorable. God ordained marriage and sex, and God said sex is good. The devil and his demons have distorted it for the world, but it's not going to be distorted for me. I married this man, and I'm going to love him, and I'm going to be the best lover."

When I first came to that knowledge, I really didn't enjoy sex, but by faith I said, "I'm going to enjoy my husband." I actually began to enjoy him. I even approached him. He thought, *Is this the same woman?*

I get great delight out of saying, "Honey, I really need you tonight," and he'll say, "Baby, I'm tired." I tell him okay. See, you ladies don't have to be the one who is tired or has a headache!

The whole theme of the above Scripture is the sexual relationship between a husband and wife. Sex brings life, and not only in the conception of children. The right stimulants before the actual sexual act can help to make intercourse more enjoyable for both partners. But we've got to learn to communicate our desires to one another.

A wife needs to ask her husband, "What do you like for me to do? What stimulates and turns you on?" She may be doing something that turns him off. How are you going to enjoy sex if you're turned off before you get into the act? The husband needs to ask his wife the same things.

You cannot let pride get in the way. You should be totally honest and open and tell each other what you like and what you do not like. Then work with what your partner likes. Don't force your selfish desires on your mate.

When you communicate like that and work together to see that both partners have their needs and desires met, then it keeps getting better and better.

• When brothers grow up with sisters, the little girls will hold and cuddle their dolls; the boys will pull the doll's head off to see how it operates.

13
You Can't Change Your Mate

We know the Word is going to make the difference. It's the Word of God that's made the difference in your life. It's not the color of your skin, not whether you're male or female, but it's the Jesus that you serve. It's His Word that you act on that makes things happen for you.

He's trying to get into our minds that if we'll reach out to Him first of all; then, we, as husband and wife, reach toward one another, and together reach toward God, there's nothing He won't do for us. We won't have to worry about our children, about our family, about our church, about our schools, our communities, our towns, our state; because it all starts with that man and wife.

If you know God, you're going to obey the Word of God.

But it depends on your faith level in God. If you have great faith in God, if you love God like you say you do, you'll do what He says. It all begins with the husband and wife relationship. The first book of the Bible begins with how God ordained husband and wife. He created male and then female and joined them together. We are a blessed people. Proverbs 12:4 says,

A virtuous woman is a crown to her husband: but she that maketh ashamed is as rottenness in his bones.

When we were in London, we had the opportunity to see some crowns in a window. Then, as we were touring the city, we were shown the building that houses all the crowns and jewels of all the kings and queens throughout British history. They are locked up under heavy security. There are guards all around.

Those jewels were locked up because they are very precious; they are priceless. If a woman is a crown to her husband, then a man ought to cherish his crown, treat his wife as something very precious, priceless. When he does that, the gems that are in her are going to radiate life. Whatever she is, she is a reflection of her husband.

But if she is a virtuous woman, a woman of integrity, with character, of grace and poise, it's because of her husband. She is the product of her husband's care for her. If she is a bitter or hateful or nagging woman, it's simply because of him. You make each other into what you are. If you are living with somebody you don't like, you need to go back to the mold. Go back to the One Who makes the pottery: God. God can mold us and reshape us.

In the early years of marriage, we had some little habits that we didn't like about each other.And we set out to change one another. The more we tried to change each other, the more each of us rebelled. We were going farther and farther apart. You can see that in children.

You cannot change a negative action with a negative reaction. You've got to change a negative characteristic with positive reinforcement. People — children and adults — are prone to respond to reinforcement through positive communication and positive gratification.

When people begin to say good things to us, it causes us to improve in our weaker areas.

Thank God for your mate. Say good things to your mate and about your mate, because the Word of God says you can have what you say. (Mark 11:23.) If your husband (or wife) is an alcoholic, a drug addict, don't say, "You are nothing but a no-good bum," because that's what you're going to have. If you begin to say, by faith, "You may be drinking today, but I see you as a saved child of God, an honor to God, a blessing in this home and community," then, you are going to have that. You will have what you say. We need to take the Word of God literally. It's true. God says in Isaiah 55:11,

> **So shall My word be that goeth forth out of My mouth: it shall not return unto Me void, but it shall accomplish that which I please, and it shall prosper in the thing whereto I sent it.**

God backs up His Word. If His Word is not working, that means that somewhere we are not working the Word. We have seen that a virtuous woman is a crown to her husband. The second part of that verse, Proverbs 12:4 says, **but she that maketh ashamed is as rottenness in his bones.**

A woman doesn't, usually, intentionally shame, embarrass, her husband. But there are times when she puts him down in front of friends, relatives, or children, and it causes rottenness to come in his bones.

At times, men act in a way that they do not deserve to be respected; they act in a way that doesn't entice their wife even to be submitted to them. But that's their problem. God commands women to obey the Word. And when they do their part, that looses the angels of

God to go on their behalf and to begin to work on that man. We've found out that as we stay in close fellowship with God, we have no problem. We have one of the greatest marriage relationships in the whole world, but we're tough to live with. Neither of us is easy to live with. We are totally different. God made us that way.

If you look at the person you're living with, you'd probably say the same thing. Sometimes the devil will tell you, "You married the wrong person." Most people marry someone who is totally opposite to them. Very seldom do you find two fussing people who marry or two talkative people who marry or two quiet people. One person is going to talk and one is going to be quiet. God did that to balance us out.

We are perfect for one another. But we only realized we were perfect for one another as we began to know how to love God. When we can love each other like we love God — unconditionally — it means we can discuss any problem or situation we have, regardless of how we feel.

When we first got married, Mack loved to keep his shoes shined. In elementary school and in high school, he used to carry a stocking cap in his pocket, and every 500 yards, he'd wipe off his shoes. When we got married, he still did it.

Somehow, the devil would get in my feet; I could be on this side of the room and somehow my feet would touch his shoes. It would rub him the wrong way. I could tell. I'd say, "I'm sorry."

"If you were sorry, you wouldn't keep doing it." It would take him a little while to get himself back together and realize he still loved me, even if I did step on his shiny shoes.

I responded to situations like that with the question in my mind, *Is this an adult, a grown man? Children act like that. Did I marry the right person?*

Little habits that each of us does causes our mate to become irritated. Some people get upset over how you squeeze the toothpaste. Some people take the middle of the tube and mash it. It makes more sense to start from the bottom and roll it up to the top. But God will give you one that squeezes it in the middle. Some people are messy. You wonder, *Why can't they pick up after themselves? They are adults.*

God put you there to pick up behind them. Because once he or she loses something, and you pick it up, they're going to realize it and thank you. One day they will catch on: every time I leave something on the floor, it gets picked up. It takes time; but when that mate can see that you love them, regardless of the little habits they have that irritate you to the bone, then you will make it.

Satan will do everything he can, little things, very simple things, to get you going. But once you realize his tactics, say, "God has given me this mate, and I love You, God, and I love my mate."

The Word of God says we're supposed to love our spouse, our best friend, as to the Lord. When we do that, it will be unconditional. We'll have more than enough love. Every time a person sees us, they'll see love. If we're happy in our home, it's going to show.

Don't fool yourself: if you have an argument or disagreement or have some problems in your home that you can't work out, that's going to show, too. James 4:8 says to, **Draw near to God, and He will draw near to you.**

As couples, we have no excuse for not walking in an abundant and a successful life. We cannot get caught up in petty differences. Our mate is not only our best friend, but together we're a powerful team for God.

God wants to do more with us than we could ever imagine, but He wants us to get hold and control of the situation we're in now.

In Matthew 25, Jesus tells a parable about a man who was going on a trip and he called his servants to him and entrusted them with his goods.

> **And unto one he gave five talents, to another two, and to another one; to every man according to his several ability; and straightway took his journey.**
>
> **Verse 15**

After a long time, he returned and asked for an accounting from his servants of what they had done with his goods. The servant who had five and the one who had two doubled their talents by wise investments. The servant who had one, in fear, buried his. When he returned the one talent to his master, the master called him wicked and lazy. Then the master said,

> **Take therefore the talent from him, and give it unto him which hath ten talents.**
>
> **For unto every one that hath shall be given, and he shall have abundance: but from him that hath not shall be taken away even that which he hath.**
>
> **Verses 28,29**

Purpose to be diligent to study and act on the Word of God in your home. Be a faithful servant so God can use you and prosper you with abundance.

You Can Change You

Every time I would go to God and complain about what Brenda was doing (or I went to Him and complained about Mack), God would always tell me what I could do to make the situation better. God will never agree with you about the faults of somebody else in a relationship. He'll always show you what you can do. And He'll usually start off by telling you and showing you how you can forgive and love more.

A miracle took place in our relationship when we stopped trying to change each other and decided to try to out love each other.

Jesus said in John chapter 15,

> These things have I spoken unto you, that My joy might remain in you, and that your joy might be full.
>
> This is My commandment, That ye love one another, as I have loved you.
>
> Greater love hath no man than this, that a man lay down his life for his friends.
>
> Ye are My friends, if ye do whatsoever I command you.
>
> **Verses 11-14**

We each decided, "I'm going to get a word from God each day that tells me how to love you." You can have unspeakable joy when you learn how to love the way God loves.

We are full of joy because we've learned some principles of how to love one another unconditionally.

We walk together as one; we are a team. Our marriage, our friendship, is not a drudgery. We're with each other 24 hours a day, and we look toward each new day with expectancy.

Look again at verse 12. **This is My commandment, That ye love one another, as I have loved you.**

How do you love your mate? Read the Bible and get before God, and He'll show you, day by day, how to do it. He'll tell you when to buy a gift, when to send a card, when to leave a love note. He'll show you how to love. You can do it. You'll have to deny yourself and spend some time loving God...loving God...loving God. That was a revelation.

• People go to the *altar* thinking they will *alter* their mate. People should go to the altar because they have accepted their mate.

14
Don't Hurt Each Other

As we look to enrich our marriage and to be a better friend to our mate, we need to understand about the needs that are common to both men and women.

It has been stated that in today's society men and women all over the world obtain education for everything but how to relate as husband and wife. We go to school for twelve years. Many go on to college for four additional years. In certain professions, it is necessary to have four years or more of training and then take tests in those particular areas. Then you have to be licensed or certified before you can actually work in that field.

But when it comes down to male and female relationships, we have couples all the time that believe God has called the two of them to be united in holy matrimony for the rest of their lives, but they do not take any course to find out how to be a husband and wife, how to work within the relationship, or how the opposite sex thinks and responds, even in the most common of situations. Therefore, most people enter into a marriage relationship ignorant.

Part of the responsibility that belongs to both the husband and the wife is to be a sensitive, caring friend to each other. Sometimes, very early in a marriage, hurts can be sustained and those wounds are not healed for years. Let's look at some of the hazards, some of the ways we hurt each other —knowingly or not — so we can avoid them. Remember, **My people are destroyed for lack of knowledge** (Hos. 4:6). This will bring you knowledge. Then you must decide to walk in it.

Very often, we hurt each other by frequently criticizing one another, finding fault.

Early in our relationship, before we got married, I was just perfect for Mack. But about three weeks after we got married, everything was wrong. I talked too much. I was too skinny for him.

Men are task-oriented: they have the goal of getting the woman. But there's not much preparation in keeping the woman. Men buy flowers all the time they are dating; they say all the right things. They are there all the time. They even think about candlelight dinners, up until that moment when they say, "I do." Then, unless they have received good Christian training, they say, "I've got her. I've achieved her," and they settle down.

It has been stated that the moment the woman and man say, "I do," in their minds they are thinking, *Boy, I'm going to change him (her). I'm going to make him (her) the way I want him (her) to be.* But before they were married, everything was perfect.

Matthew 22:36,37 says,

> **Master, which is the great commandment in the law?**
>
> **Jesus said unto him, Thou shalt love the Lord thy God with all thy heart, and with all thy soul, and with all thy mind.**

If you love somebody with all your heart, soul, and mind, that's your total being.

God says that we need to love Him with our whole being. Until we can love God with our whole being, we won't be able to understand how to love one another. When you love God with your total being, you ache for God.

Many times, if you have lost loved ones, maybe moms and dads or brothers and sisters or close friends, at those moments, because you've lost someone you care for, your heart aches. Your heart literally aches, because your spirit is grieved that you won't have fellowship with them anymore. It doesn't mean you won't remember them, but you won't have fellowship. When we don't have fellowship with God, the spirit within us that is of God aches for God.

There are times we have heartaches, but we blame other people. We blame our mate, or children, or co-workers or people who hurt us; and we say we have a heartache. But if we truly love God, the love that is shed abroad in our hearts will give us such a love that our heart won't have to ache. (Rom. 5:5.)

We don't have to have broken hearts, because God sent Jesus to mend the brokenhearted. (Luke 4:18.)

Jesus said, **I will never leave thee, nor forsake thee** (Heb. 13:5). We are never alone. We will never have to have another lonely day in our life. **I will never leave you comfortless: I will come to you** (John 14:18).

As a young girl, growing up, the devil had convinced me that I was so alone. Even though I had people around me, I was so alone. But the Word of God now tells me that I'm never alone. It upsets me knowing the number of years that I wasted, having pity parties, believing the things that the devil tried to tell me. But thank God, He opened up my eyes. Don't waste any time having pity parties.

Jesus Is the Seed

Verily, verily, I say unto you, Except a corn of wheat fall into the ground and die, it abideth alone: but if it die, it bringeth forth much fruit.

John 12:24

In order for something to be produced, something has to die. When Jesus died, He was the seed that God planted in this earth.

When you put a seed in the ground it germinates, but it dies first. Then it germinates and begins to grow from the moisture of the soil. With the right substance in the soil, and the water and sunshine, that seed begins to produce a crop.

If we will plant our lives in Him, the Word says, in Him we live, in Him we move, and in Him we have our being. (Acts 17:28.) Unless we are in Him, we won't move or live, and we won't have a being, because it will be controlled by the devil. We have to plant our feet on solid ground and remind ourselves that we are rooted and grounded and established in the Word of God. Since Jesus said in Matthew 22:37 for us to love the Lord our God with all our heart, with all our soul, and with all our mind, it must be something that can be done. How? Pray, even as you're reading this, "Father God, give me the ability and give me the knowing within my spirit that I love You with all my heart, and give me the ability to love You with all my soul, and, Father, give me the ability, daily, to love You with all my mind."

We have no excuse to not walk in perfect peace. When evil thoughts come to you about your mate, the one you are supposed to love as you love yourself, remind yourself that it is a lie from the devil and take control over it.

Put your hand on your mind. Say, "Mind, you are going to be controlled by the Word of God. I cast down every vain and every evil imagination that will try to exalt itself against the Word of God. I cast it down in the name of Jesus. I'm taking control over you. I will not entertain evil thoughts, in Jesus' name."

Every day you have to talk to yourself like that, because the Word says He will keep you in perfect peace if your mind is stayed on Him. (Isa. 26:3.) If you are not walking in perfect peace, it's simply because your mind is not on God.

Paul said, "I keep my body under control daily." (1 Cor. 9:27.) God doesn't want us to bruise our body, but He wants us to do whatever it takes to keep our spirit, soul, and body stayed on Him.

A lot of times our body needs to be buffeted. That means it needs to do something that it doesn't necessarily want to do. We don't necessarily want to get up in the morning and praise God. The body wants to lay in that bed and be defeated another day. But the Word of God will tell that mind, "Control this body and make it get up and begin to praise and worship God." That is where your strength comes from. Your gasoline is your praise and worship.

Your car is not going anywhere without gasoline. And you are not going anywhere without praying in the Holy Ghost. Praying in the Holy Ghost is what keeps relationships intact. You must keep your mind on God, love Him with all your being and control your body and soul with the Word of God before you will have any significant degree of success in loving, and not hurting, your mate.

Look at Ephesians 4:32.

And be ye kind one to another, tenderhearted, forgiving one another, even as God for Christ's sake hath forgiven you.

If we are like Jesus, we are supposed to be tenderhearted. Tenderhearted means the heart is gentle, compassionate toward one another. A tenderhearted person is a person who has mercy. A merciful person is a person who is longsuffering. A longsuffering person is a person who is forgiving. A forgiving person is a person who always looks at the good side of a person. And the list goes on and on...until you find no fault.

In order for our relationship to be strong, we have to move like Jesus. Jesus is tenderhearted and moves with compassion. When we mess up with God, He is always gentle toward us when we come to Him and ask forgiveness. He always says, "Come. I stand with open arms, ready to forgive and welcome you back into fellowship." That is the attitude we are supposed to have when our mate messes up, when our best friend hurts us. Jesus gave us a clear example in the story of the prodigal son.

The story is found in Luke 15 beginning in verse 11.

And he said, A certain man had two sons:

And the younger of them said to his father, Father, give me the portion of goods that falleth to me. And he divided unto them his living.

And not many days after the younger son gathered all together, and took his journey into a far country, and there wasted his substance with riotous living...

And when he came to himself, he said, How many hired servants of my father's have bread enough and to spare, and I perish with hunger!

I will arise and go to my father, and will say unto him, Father, I have sinned against heaven, and before thee...

And he arose, and came to his father. But when he was yet a great way off, his father saw him, and had compassion, and ran, and fell on his neck, and kissed him...

And bring hither the fatted calf, and kill it; and let us eat, and be merry:

For this my son was dead, and is alive again; he was lost, and is found. And they began to be merry.

Verses 11-13,17,18,20,23,24

Our Heavenly Father is never harsh with us. He always welcomes us back with open arms.

Look at the older brother in this story.

Now his elder son was in the field: and as he came and drew nigh to the house, he heard music and dancing.

And he called one of the servants, and asked what these things meant.

And he said unto him, Thy brother is come; and thy father hath killed the fatted calf, because he hath received him safe and sound.

And he was angry, and would not go in....

Verses 25-28

Too often, instead of following the example of the father in this story, we are like the older brother, unforgiving. We think we are so perfect, sometimes. None of us are perfect, but we are reaching toward perfection when we begin to treat each other with kindness, affection, and forgiveness.

When you feel yourself getting mad at your friend, you better pray in the Holy Ghost. As you submit to God, by praying in the Holy Ghost, the Holy Ghost will take control. It's the power of the Holy Ghost that keeps us. He begins to water down those impurities. We're washed and purified and cleansed through the Word of God. (Eph. 5:26.)

We also hurt each other when we ignore one another.

Don't let the television, the newspaper, or anything else take your attention when your best friend wants to talk to you. We must esteem one another, count them as valuable.

There was an article about a woman who, crying hysterically, called her daughter on the telephone. The daughter asked, "What's wrong, Mama?"

The mother answered, "I've got to come over. I need $450.00."

"Why?"

"Because I blew up your daddy's television. I got mad because he kept watching the television, and I took the hammer and hit in the front of it."

"But, Mama, you could have gotten electrocuted," said the daughter.

"I was so mad I didn't realize that! Then your dad got up and went into the den and turned on the television in there."

Men, when a woman is mad enough to hit a television, you better say, "What do you want?"

Another area that can become a source of hurt is if each partner does not assume enough responsibility.

Sometimes, the man believes that if he goes out and works and brings in his paycheck that he's done all he's supposed to do. His wife, he feels, ought to be grateful that he shows up at home. But no, men have more responsibility than only to bring home the paycheck, particularly now with women working and bringing home a paycheck, too.

So, if a man comes home with that attitude, very likely no cooking will get done; no cleaning will get done — nothing will get done. The best thing to do is decide who is going to do what. Where does it say that the woman is supposed to do all the ironing? In our house, we both do it.

A husband is helping himself when he helps his wife. If he does some of the work, then she can be full of energy when all the chores are done. She can be lying in bed, just waiting for him. That's a smart man.

When you step through the door, begin to be attentive to the things around you and see what your partner needs. If both husband and wife are working, when you come home discuss what needs to be done, and work together to get it done. We've got to be sensitive to one another.

It can hurt your mate if it seems that his or her desires are secondary to the other one's activities: in other words, if you're too busy doing whatever you're doing to do what the other person needs.

Whenever your husband or wife asks you to do something, make that a priority. There isn't anything more important than fulfilling a mate's desire. Usually, the spouse only asks because it seems as though the other person isn't doing anything more important than what needs to be done. The need appears to be a priority.

For instance, if I'm in the house sitting around doing nothing and Mack says, "Why don't we clean the car? Brenda, I need you to wash the windows."

If I say, "I'm not washing any windows; I'm busy," that's not being a good mate. A true friend will desire to be out there helping him wash the windows, because he asked me.

Then, when we come in the house, if she needs help and asks, "Honey, would you clean the den while I finish bathing the children," as a good mate, I say, "Sure, Brenda, no problem."

The way you correct mistakes and faults and avoid hurts in a relationship is...by doing it. If you want a person to become more sensitive to you, you have to become more sensitive to them.

There are many men who enjoy watching sports: football, basketball, wrestling, boxing. Many women do not enjoy that pastime. But if it is something your husband enjoys, and you enjoy being with your husband, you'll learn to like them too, if for no other reason than because it allows you to be with him. If sitting beside your mate doesn't bring you joy, you're in trouble.

Look for ways to be together. Try to out love each other. When we were having many problems in our relationship, we literally decided we were going to out love each other. Each of us decided we were going to be the very best we could be. We daily try to out give each other. But it can't be done. Just like you can't out give God. The more you give to God, the more He returns to you.

Why is that? Because God says,

> **Give, and it shall be given unto you; good measure, pressed down, and shaken together, and running over, shall men give into your bosom. For with the same measure that ye mete withal it shall be measured to you again.**
>
> **Luke 6:38**

The more we give to our mate, the more our mate is free to give to us. God says be a blessing, and you will be blessed.

This is important: never leave one another with negative words or anger. When you get ready to depart from one another, whether he's going to work or just out to wash the car, make sure you're at peace with one another and you have ministered words of love to your mate.

We heard a testimony the other day of a wife who said she and her husband had spoken terrible words to one another. "It was so horrible," she said. "I'll never forget that conversation. It was the last time I saw him alive. He left while we were still angry at each other and was killed in an accident." Don't ever leave angry at one another.

It's easy to get angry, because we are built differently, and we think totally different, as we have already discussed. We respond to things in totally different ways. That's why Paul wrote the letter in Colossians 3. If you, as a man, don't understand that you're going to move or respond to something totally different than your wife, you'll get so mad at her; then, you'll be walking around and your prayers won't get answered and you won't know why.

Colossians 3:19 says, **Husbands, love your wives, and be not bitter against them.** Here's a command from the Word of God. Don't be bitter against them. Men and women respond differently in many situations. God made us that way to keep us both praying and to keep us sensitive to one another. Remember, men are task-oriented. Women respond through their emotions.

Men can get mad. (Women can, too.) They may bark, "Come here." The woman then gets angry and upset. You need to understand that God made us different to keep a balance in our relationships. Don't return anger for anger. A soft word turns away wrath. (Prov. 15:1.)

There's not a home that can't be happy, if you make up your mind you're going to hear the right way. You can be angry but sin not. (Eph. 4:26.)

How can you be angry and not sin?

Say, "Honey, forgive me. I didn't mean to say that." Those are some of the hardest words to get out of our mouth. Demonstrate your caring by your actions. Words won't be enough. You're going to have to *do* something. God didn't stop at saying, "I love you," then send us back to that slave block and let the devil get us. He acted. He sent His Son. His Son came and destroyed the works of the devil. Love will always act.

Husbands, share your moments of weakness and times of failure with your wife. She already knows. She's waiting for you to say it. She has some of the best instruction to counsel you. But you are "such a man," and you know how to punch out people, so she keeps her mouth shut. Share your moments of weakness and failures. And then shut up and listen to the counsel that comes through. Share it. Let her know that your life would not be complete without her.

Let her know. Say, "Honey, my life would not be nearly as happy without you. I'm so happy I didn't marry the wrong person." Life is too short to be miserable.

It is important, and it will help to avoid hurt in your relationship, if you will reinforce to your mate that he (or she) is more valuable than your job, your mama, your friends, and even your children.

We need men who know how to make sure their wife knows she is in first place, above their mama. Men need to cut the umbilical cord. It's time for you to grow up. The Bible told you to leave your father and your mother and cleave to your wife. (Matt. 19:5.) You may have the greatest parents in the world, but your wife better take first place. You're not a godly man if your wife doesn't take first place.

If a husband sees that his wife is sad, he should ask her, "What's wrong, honey?" He should not give up until he finds out. If it happens that the husband is the problem, sometimes he gets offended.

"What do you mean, I'm the problem?"

"You didn't even remember our anniversary. Your boss could call you down to the pool room but you don't have time to take me out."

"Didn't I tell you I loved you when I married you?" Just like your body needs a good bath every day, your marriage relationship needs to be washed in the Word of God, daily.

• One wrong word can destroy a relationship. One right word can bond two lives together.

15

Treasure Your Relationship

In the marriage relationship sometimes a husband and wife unintentionally hurt each other. They can forgive one another, but sometimes they are still hurt because of the damage that has been done. There's a long process to healing. Words are not enough. Women are also moved by actions. Even after you say, "I'm sorry," it takes a long time for a woman to heal. That's where patience has to be developed inside of men. A woman is thinking, *Sure, you said that last time.* Patience and action.

It's the fear of God and the reverence of God that makes a man want to know more about how to treat his wife, because he knows he will have to give an account of how he treated her to her spiritual Father, Eternal God.

In the beginning, it's a matter of deciding to seek after knowledge so we can carry out this lifestyle that God wants in our relationship. But look at Matthew 6:21, **For where your treasure is, there will your heart be also.**

God wants you to love Him, but loving Him is different than doing His work. He wants you to love Him, fellowship with Him, and worship Him. He desires for you to take time to have conversations with Him. But then, in the marriage relationship, your first ministry to God is your mate.

Your spouse should be number one, under God, over everything else. Your mate should be your priority over your job, your car, your relatives, your church, everything.

Although God is first in our individual lives, when we come together, our mates should be priority over anything. Yet, it seems when you get married, everything else is priority.

Many couples, even in the church, have their relationships out of order. They have their jobs as their first priority, then their friends, relatives, or children. Those are all important, but they are not as important as their mate. We even see some people put the work of the ministry above their marriage.

That is how I was in 1979. God spoke to me and said, "Mack, your priorities in life are wrong." I had put the work of the ministry before my relationship with Brenda, my friend and life partner. I had allowed the ministry to become more important than my wife. The reason that happened was our communication was not good, and we had come into conflict. We were at the point of disagreement. It was easier for me to concentrate my effort in the work of the ministry.

But the time came when I told my husband, "Mack, I need your attention. I need you here with me." I had become very angry with the ministry. Every time we had a day to ourselves, there was something going on at the church. It makes the wife resentful.

If the husband has a day at home, and the wife is over at some club meeting with the girls or even at home on the telephone all night, the husband could be resentful. You have to have a serious talk.

It takes time and faith and patience to be honest with one another and to work together to get the priorities straightened out.

Why? Because when you come together, at first, you develop a relationship of conflict. You are prone to run away from conflict, so you avoid one another. (That's what I was doing by concentrating all my time in the church!) We find a lot of couples, especially ladies, hold a lot in. They don't feel their husband will listen when they say something; or they feel he will lash out physically or verbally. Some men call their wives stupid. They tell her, "You're just like a child." Women don't need to hear things like that.

But there are times you do have to meet or talk about things which are not really comfortable.

When these times come, you have to learn to shut your mouth and not defend yourself. You have to become really good listeners.

Sometimes we don't say things the way we mean them so, rather than cutting them off in the middle of what they're saying, we have to ask questions like, "Is this what you're trying to say?" That way your partner knows you are trying to get the meaning.

Couples tell us, "We're tired of living a lie. We come to church every Sunday, and we hear you minister, but we can't get together in the home."

This is why many people want to stay in church all the time. It doesn't take any effort to sit together in church. When you go home is where the real test comes into focus. You have to communicate; put the Word into practice. Couples will come home from church and tell each other, "You heard what the preacher said this morning. You're supposed to...." If you were both doing what you're *supposed* to do, this wouldn't happen.

The basic reason is they have not developed their relationship with Jesus Christ. When you develop your relationship with Jesus, He'll talk with you, counsel you, give you His ability to love and forgive, His ability to understand. He'll show you how to treasure your mate.

Every week, the husband and wife should set aside time to sit down and discuss serious issues. They should talk about how they feel, what they need, what they want. Be completely honest with each other. Then brace yourselves for the response that may come.

There came a point in our life when we knew we had to get honest with one another. That took a lot.

There was a time that I was afraid to really express how I felt to my husband, because I felt like he would put me down.

And I was afraid to express how I felt to Brenda, because I felt it would put a gap between us. And initially, it will. But if you are men and women of God, God will bridge that gap. But you've got to start being honest and trustworthy with one another.

We began to share with one another. I began to tell Mack what I wanted in a man, what I *needed* as a woman.

I began to share with Brenda what I *needed* as a husband, and what I wanted in a wife.

We said, "Okay." We saw areas that we were falling short in, and we purposed to improve in those areas. It doesn't mean that you are a failure, or you're a mistake; it means you are maturing. You're no less of a man and no less of a woman. It means that we are mature enough to say, "We're going to improve. Our marriage is going to be better. We're going to have heaven on earth." Until you purpose to do that, you won't.

It takes mature people to be able to sit down, discuss your differences and learn to bridge these differences.

At least once each week, we'll ask each other, "Are there areas in my life where I need to improve? Are there things that I'm not doing that you need me to do? Are there areas where I'm not meeting your needs?"

Take time to review where you are, personally. Make sure you're walking in love with the wonderful mate God has given you. Walking in love is walking in forgiveness.

For where your treasure is.... Where is your treasure? Do you treasure your mate?

When your wife is hurting or upset, do you cast her aside or say, "You're a cry baby. All you do is cry, cry, cry"? Or do you try to find out why she cries so much? There are emotional stresses that affect a woman but will go unnoticed by a man. But if he values his wife, he'll offer her his shoulder rather than his mouth. She needs his comfort, not a lecture.

When your husband finally puts up the curtains or shines the floor — tasks you may have asked him to do weeks before — do you even notice? A man needs instant gratification; he needs to know he is appreciated. Take the time and show him.

A woman bases the value of your relationship on the amount of time you spend with her. Ask her, "Do you feel like there is anything pertaining to my job or some of my friends or anything I'm doing that is more valuable to me than you?" Be sure to tell her what you're doing.

The best thing a man can do is have a good conversation with his wife when he first gets home and let her know everything. Women want to know every little detail. "Who did you see?" And if you saw somebody that you both know, she wants to know how they looked, how many children they have, where they live — everything.

If the husband has taken out time for his wife, and demonstrated to her that he prizes her, she will be more understanding and free up time for him to do extra things.

When your partner receives and believes that you are truly committed and really care, they'll even start suggesting you do some things that you wanted to do but have not made time for in the past. When Brenda sees that I really care about her as a person, and not as an object, she'll say things like, "Honey, you go ahead and do (whatever), because I know you've been wanting to do that."

But that's not going to happen if you are not sensitive to meet her needs. She knows she is my treasure.

When you see a treasure, a wise person will make an investment in it. Sometimes the investment is saying, "I care about you. Could we have lunch together?" Or, "How would you like to go to a movie?"

If you invest in treasure that is not already being taken care of, you're going to get the dividends.

As a wife, I purpose to do something special for my husband every day. In turn, he does something special for me. Maybe I'll leave a note on the bathroom mirror saying, "You're the greatest husband in the world. I love you." Mack likes chocolate with nuts or coconuts. I sometimes leave a candy bar on the pillow for him. Whenever I go shopping, whether it's getting groceries or buying clothes for the kids, I always think about my husband. If I don't get anything but a handkerchief, I bring it to let him know that Dad was thought about.

Sometimes, I'll tell Brenda, "Let's go out for lunch."

And she says, "Sure, where do you want to go?"

Then I tell my friend, my treasure, "It doesn't matter, as long as I'm with you."

We have times with the children, but sometimes we go out to dinner, just the two of us. It's worth getting a babysitter. Our time together is valuable.

Watch everything in your life begin to take on a new energy and a positive direction when you major on your relationship with your mate.

Your treasure is worth the investment of your time and your finances. Mack caught on to that at a time when our finances were tight. He bought me a nightgown that you could see through. You could feel the wind through it. I asked him, "How much did you pay for this thing?"

"Forty-two dollars," he said.

I said, "I could have bought a dress with that." But then the Holy Spirit touched me, and I realized I was glad I was the one Mack had chosen to be his wife and given this present to, so I put that thing on, breeze and all!

There were times we didn't have any extra money to put out and Brenda would go to the time and trouble to cook my favorite meals. She would cook fried chicken, potato salad, garden peas, hot rolls, and coconut pie. Then she would put a cloth on the table, and cloth napkins, and turn down the lights. We would have dinner for two, and it was the finest restaurant we could have ever gone to.

There are times a lady wants to go out and eat, and we have heard some men say, "You cook just as good as they do at the restaurant. Besides, we're already running tight, and I can use that money to buy groceries."

Perhaps your wife is an elegant gourmet cook. But sometimes, she wants to be in another environment besides her home. She needs a change of scenery. And she needs to see that she is worth the investment of your time and money.

We have found out in our own personal lives, as we purpose to minister to one another, and we get together, particularly on a budget, God opens up the way so we have extra finances. Your mate is worth the investment.

Men get gratification from achievement; that's why they are so goal-oriented. They have the desire to go out and conquer. Go get the trophy; be the winner. Get the promotion on the job. A loving wife can invest praise and admiration in her man and receive a bountiful return on her investment.

Women get their happiness and fulfillment when the relationship with her family is right.

Proverbs 31 tells us,

> **Who can find a virtuous woman? for her price is far above rubies.**
>
> **The heart of her husband doth safely trust in her, so that he shall have no need of spoil.**
>
> **She will do him good and not evil all the days of her life.**
>
> **Verses 10-12**

This is the treasure in which God tells husbands to invest.

It's easy to see if a woman is being cared for, because it shows in her face. There is life in her cheeks when she's happy. There is a sparkle in her eyes. It shows; it's there. When she is not happy, it also shows.

Verses 28,29:

> **Her children arise up, and call her blessed; her husband also, and he praiseth her.**
>
> **Many daughters have done virtuously, but thou excellest them all.**

It says that her children rise up and call her blessed. If the children never say, "Mama, thank you for hemming my pants; thank you for ironing my dress; Mama that meal was good;" she is going to be down in her spirit.

147

Husbands need to be sensitive to the way children treat Mama. The woman does many things; a "thank you" is a small thing to invest in such a treasure.

The husband is the head of the relationship between the husband and wife. When you're the head of something, you have to have knowledge of many things. The husband must have knowledge of what makes the family operate. He must see that the children appreciate everything their mama does for them, but then he needs to realize, he also needs to praise her. Every day a husband should say the things to his wife that he said before they got married. Every day you have to put more into that woman's spirit about how much you love her.

If you have a wife who cries a lot or is down, tired, and drained, it may be the words that you are saying or the lack of praise that she's receiving from her children. When a female is not appreciated, she gets drained. When you tell a lady, "That was a good meal; I appreciate it," it puts energy into her. When you tell her she looks good, it puts energy in her. You may want to evaluate the investment you've been making with your words.

In order for your relationship as friends and as marriage partners to prosper, you've got to walk in love and forgiveness. And you've got to let all bitterness, wrath, and anger cease from your life. It is the voice of the flesh that screams at us when our mate has hurt us, "Get him back." There are many times that voice has spoken to me, and I really wanted to get Mack back.

Sometimes she did.

Then there were other times I thought of things I could do. But the Holy Spirit would say, "No, don't do that." But there are times in all of our lives when we have that burning desire to get even. But it's only the Holy Spirit that quenches that desire and love overrides that. But whatever is the greater one in you, that's what you're going to be drawn to. If the flesh is greater, you're going to be drawn and moved by the flesh. But if the Spirit of God is greater, you're going to be moved with compassion, love, and forgiveness.

Be ye therefore followers of God, as dear children;

And walk in love, as Christ also hath loved us, and hath given Himself for us an offering and a sacrifice to God for a sweetsmelling savor.

Ephesians 5:1,2

When you think about it, why would you really ever want to hurt your very best friend, your treasure, your spouse?

• Every day you have with your mate is a day you will never have again.

16
Sing the Song of Songs

In concluding this book on being married and friends, we want to take a few pages to share with you some things Solomon said to his wife. This is going to get romantic!

She was a young girl who was brought in to keep David warm, when he was very old. She was a virgin and David never knew her sexually. Solomon later married this girl.

We'll begin in chapter 4.

Behold, thou art fair, my love; behold, thou art fair; thou hast doves' eyes within thy locks: thy hair is as a flock of goats, that appear from mount Gilead.

Verse 1

Husbands, you say that to your wife. There are not many women who can stand against that kind of talk if they're feeling it with your eyes and in the softness of your voice.

He is telling her, "You are fair"; in other words, she is beautiful.

Then he talks about her eyes. When you love someone, you look into their eyes. Obviously, he had looked at a dove before; normally, a dove is considered a very peaceable, calming bird. Her eyes calmed him.

Solomon continued,

> Thy teeth are like a flock of sheep that are even shorn, which came up from the washing; whereof every one bear twins, and none is barren among them.

> Thy lips are like a thread of scarlet, and thy speech is comely: thy temples are like a piece of a pomegranate within thy locks.

> Thy neck is like the tower of David builded for an armoury, whereon there hang a thousand bucklers, all shields of mighty men.

> Thou art all fair, my love; there is no spot in thee.
>
> **Verses 2-4,7**

Are you getting the picture? This man was looking closely at her and he liked what he saw. And he *told* her. "My love, there is no spot in thee." Nobody is perfect; but to him, she was the most beautiful woman in the world.

She had fallen asleep in chapter 5. He had come home a little later than usual, and he tried to get in the door but she had it latched. Look what she says.

> My beloved put in his hand by the hole of the door, and my bowels were moved for him.
>
> **Verse 4**

She just saw his hands and she was moved on the inside. She was half asleep, but she saw his hand and rose up to open the door. She was too late.

> I opened to my beloved; but my beloved had withdrawn himself, and was gone: my soul failed when he spake: I sought him, but I could not find him; I called him, but he gave me no answer...

> My beloved is white and ruddy, the chiefest among ten thousand.

His head is as the most fine gold, his locks are bushy, and black as a raven.

His eyes are as the eyes of doves by the rivers of waters, washed with milk, and fitly set.

His cheeks are as a bed of spices, as sweet flowers: his lips like lilies, dropping sweet smelling myrrh.

His hands are as gold rings set with the beryl: his belly is as bright ivory overlaid with sapphires.

His legs are as pillars of marble, set upon sockets of fine gold: his countenance is as Lebanon, excellent as the cedars.

His mouth is most sweet: yea, he is altogether lovely. This is my beloved, and this is my friend, O daughters of Jerusalem.

Verses 6,10-16

Look how her words build him up. He is the most handsome man in the world to her. His physical attributes are very appealing. His hands turn her on. His eyes, like hers, are doves' eyes. And his mouth is most sweet. He speaks kindly to her. And look what she calls him: **this is my friend!**

It has always been God's plan for husband and wife to be married and friends.

• Remember: you can't love horizontally until you learn how to love vertically.

To contact the authors,
write:

Mack and Brenda Timberlake
Christian Faith Center
P. O. Box 100
Creedmoor, North Carolina 27522
Telephone: (919) 582-1581

Additional copies of this book are available
from your local bookstore or from:

Harrison House
P. O. Box 35035
Tulsa, Oklahoma 74153

In Canada contact:

Word Alive
P. O. Box 284
Niverville, Manitoba
CANADA R0A 1E0

The Harrison House Vision

Proclaiming the truth and power
Of the Gospel of Jesus Christ
With excellence;

Challenging Christians to
Live victoriously,
Grow spiritually,
Know God intimately.